FIX IT WITH FOOD

EVERY MEAL EASY

FIX IT WITH FOOD

EVERY MEAL EASY

Michael Symon

and Douglas Trattner

Photographs by Ed Anderson

CLARKSON POTTER/PUBLISHERS
New York

THIS COOKBOOK IS DEDICATED TO PAP, MY GRANDFATHER.

We were blessed to have him in our lives until he passed away at the age of 102. He was a daily inspiration to me, my family, and everybody who knew him. I love you, Pap.

CONTENTS

INTRODUCTION

As many of you might be aware, I suffer from two autoimmune diseases: discoid lupus and rheumatoid arthritis. I learned about these issues when I was in my twenties, but like most young people, I chose to ignore the symptoms and continued to live my life as if nothing had changed. For the most part, I was able to do so, working through the inevitable inflammation, discomfort, and pain that resulted from my poor decisions. But as I got older, the pain increased; either that or my tolerance for it declined. Regardless, something had to change.

That's when I took a very close look at my diet to see if I couldn't manage or reduce much of that discomfort simply by avoiding certain foods. On *The Chew*, I designed a 20-day food plan—what I now call the Reset—to try and zero in on which types of foods caused me inflammation (the source of my pain). The process I devised for myself consisted of a very strict diet that eliminated the most likely sources of discomfort, namely flour, dairy, meat, and sugar. By identifying and avoiding all of these so-called triggers, I found that I was largely able to stop reaching into the medicine cabinet. After sharing on TV what I learned throughout the process, I received a groundswell of positive feedback from viewers. As I was posting these recipes on social media, people were responding enthusiastically about how the Reset was helping them deal with their own triggers. That response is what encouraged me to write *Fix It with Food*, my first cookbook geared to anti-inflammatory foods and recipes. In that book we created a 10-Day Reset—along with 130 additional amazing recipes—to help people identify and manage inflammation and discomfort issues.

That book proved more successful than I could have hoped or anticipated. Obviously, I was thrilled with the sales numbers and best-seller lists, but more than that, I was delighted that a book I wrote was helping people feel better. That they could do so while preparing and enjoying delicious foods with and for their families made it all the better.

But I also learned, by listening to comments from home cooks who purchased the book, that there were things about *Fix It with Food* that could be improved upon. One of the most common topics of discussion was the serving size of the recipes. While we assumed that entire families would be embarking on this journey together, that typically wasn't the case. What we discovered from readers was that recipes built for one or two people made more sense. If you do happen to be cooking for a larger crowd—or simply want to guarantee some delicious leftovers—these recipes are easily doubled or tripled. We have even included a Useful Conversions chart (page 250) to help simplify the scaling-up process. I have always found that it's easier to multiply recipe size than to reduce it.

Another topic that frequently came up was whether the Reset recipes had to be eaten in the order that they appeared in the book, and if favorite recipes can be repeated during the process. The answers are "no" and "yes": You can enjoy any recipe within the Reset as often as you'd like and in any order you desire. I know that many people appreciate variety, so we provide enough great recipes that you can enjoy a different dish for breakfast, lunch, and dinner throughout the entire 10 days. That said, if you want to eat the same breakfast every single day for all 10 days, have at it!

Also new to this cookbook is a Master Substitution List (page 11), a handy reference guide that gives home cooks more flexibility and control when it comes to preparing meals. I know there will be times when you lack a certain ingredient—or simply don't love one that is called for in a recipe—so I offer a list of suitable replacements. I think it will make mealtime less stressful and more enjoyable.

In this book, along with a whole new 10-Day Reset of 30 recipes, I take the trigger conversation a step further and explain *how* to reintroduce ingredients—aka the triggers—into your eating routine after the Reset. This step is crucial to determining which foods can safely be enjoyed and which ones need to be avoided to keep inflammation at bay. For example, if you've eaten a flour-free, dairy-free, meat-free, sugar-free, and alcohol-free diet for the last ten days, how do you begin to introduce dairy or wheat flour back into your food to figure out if it's the culprit of your suffering? We wanted to make this process as clear and easy as possible, so I added an entire chapter (page 64) devoted to the reintroduction process.

Not surprisingly, one of the most common questions people asked me regarding the process was "What about snacks?!" So throughout this cookbook, we included mindful snacks for those who feel the urge to nosh between meals while still avoiding certain triggers. We also made sure that all the recipes—snacks and otherwise—are quick and easy enough to make so you can get breakfast, lunch, or dinner on the table in no time.

Remember, this isn't a diet book. The goal isn't to cut calories, carbs, or fat. The purpose of this cookbook—and the original *Fix It with Food*—is to give you the tools to identify your personal inflammation triggers and then to provide healthy, delicious recipes that avoid those foods. By doing so, you will likely enjoy a life with less pain. And if you happen to fall off the wagon for a meal, a day, or even two, don't panic. Everything will be okay. I am human just like everybody else. I slip and eat foods that I know are going to hurt me the next day, especially during the holidays, when it seems like I'm navigating a quagmire of sugar and dairy. (Ice cream, a double whammy in that regard, will always be my kryptonite.) The key is to stay positive and get back on track. So, happy eating! I honestly hope that all of you can achieve the balance and well-being you deserve.

The Big 30

As you cook your way through this book, it will become clear that we rely heavily on a very intentional shopping bag of ingredients. That's by design. These particular foods—what we like to call The Big 30—are superfoods when it comes to fighting inflammation. It doesn't take a nutritionist to appreciate that whole foods—foods that are more or less in their natural state—are the keys to living a better, heathier lifestyle. Leafy greens, colorful fruits and vegetables, fatty wild-caught fish, whole grains, nuts and seeds, and spices such as turmeric, ginger, and garlic not only are loaded with vitamins, minerals, and fiber, but most are known to combat the causes of inflammation.

As you familiarize yourself with the recipes in this book and move on to creating recipes of your own, keep this list as a handy guide. The more frequently you can incorporate these foods into your daily diet, the better you will feel.

1. Blueberries
2. Pineapple
3. Apples
4. Cherries
5. Oats
6. Ginger
7. Green tea
8. Wild-caught salmon
9. Red bell pepper
10. Beets
11. Broccoli
12. Beans
13. Tomatoes
14. Dark leafy greens
15. Turmeric
16. Chia seeds
17. Whole grains
18. Garlic
19. Nuts
20. Tuna packed in olive oil
21. Rosemary
22. Raw honey
23. Miso
24. Sweet potatoes
25. Mushrooms
26. Avocado
27. Jalapeño
28. Zucchini
29. Coconut oil
30. Mushroom broth

Master Substitution List

One of the most rewarding things to come out of the challenging pandemic situation was the birth of Symon's Dinners. These live-cooking segments were self-shot in my home kitchen and received more than 30 million views. Almost daily, I prepared an approachable meal while answering questions from viewers in real time. Because I wanted to make these recipes as user-friendly as possible, I designed them around common home-pantry staples combined with a few fresh vegetables and proteins. Even then, it became obvious that not everyone had access to the same ingredients. Other viewers simply didn't like a specific food, say beets or bell peppers, and didn't hesitate to voice their opinions!

So I created substitution guides as a way to empower home cooks to have more control over recipes while building confidence in their cooking practices. I didn't want someone who might not love navy beans to turn his or her nose up at an otherwise appealing recipe just because they're in there. Thanks to these guides, people felt comfortable swapping in various components that they had on hand or simply preferred. The overwhelming feedback I got was that it gave people more flexibility, control, and satisfaction.

Whenever you feel like making a swap, simply pick any ingredient from the same category. Or go crazy and mix and match, adding a little of this and a little of that. In time, through trial and error, you'll discover what works best for you, your family, and your health.

GREENS
Swiss chard
Spinach
Kale
Mustard greens
Escarole

BEANS
Black
Cannellini
Kidney
Chickpeas
Navy

ROOT VEGETABLES
Carrot
Celery root
Parsnip
Turnip
Beet

POTATOES
Sweet
Russet
Yukon Gold
Red

GRAINS
Brown rice
Quinoa
Jasmine rice
Wild rice
Oats
Arborio rice

PEPPERS
Red bell
Green bell
Yellow bell
Poblano
Cubanelle

MILKS
Cow
Oat
Soy
Almond
Cashew
Coconut

GROUND MEAT
Beef
Pork
Chicken
Turkey
Sausage of choice

SOFT SUGARS
Raw honey
Pure maple syrup
Coconut sugar
Agave

NUTS
Almonds
Cashews
Pistachios
Walnuts

10-DAY RESET

Breakfasts

Lunches

Dinners

After the release of *Fix It with Food,* we were thrilled to watch the response of enthusiastic readers, many of whom shared their progress on social media. I also published my own personal Reset journey, cooking my way through 10 days of clean eating while posting the videos online.

From experience, I know that many people prefer things spelled out for them. That's why, in the first book, we designed a 10-day menu of breakfasts, lunches, and dinners for home cooks to follow. But one of the most frequent questions that popped up surrounding the Reset process was whether someone could deviate from the routine or if there was room for modification. There is room—and you are free to chart your own course. The goal of the Reset is to exclude all potential triggers for 10 days so that you can embark on the reintroduction phase of the process to figure out which ingredients activate your inflammation. All of these recipes can be used interchangeably. So if there's a breakfast recipe that you really enjoy, go ahead and make it again. And again. If you want to prepare lunch for breakfast and dinner for lunch, there is no objective reason why you shouldn't. Every single one of these dishes is trigger-free, so they are all fair game. For this book, we decided to reorganize the Reset recipes into sections for each meal so it wouldn't appear so rigid.

My goal is twofold: first, to provide you with the information, tips, and recipes that will help you feel better and give you control over your well-being; second, to encourage you to enjoy cooking so that you'll do it more often. Find and follow a routine that works best for you and your body. Just because you've finished the 10-day Reset doesn't mean you can't ever return to these recipes. Personally, I find it helpful every three or four months to revisit the Reset because it puts me in a positive, mindful eating mode; it forces me to be more aware of what I'm eating. You don't have to do the entire 10 days; even just a day or two helps to reinforce good eating habits. Short of that, there's nothing stopping you from incorporating individual recipes into your daily or weekly routines. For example, I always have overnight oats (see page 22) in my fridge and can't seem to stay away from the Tuna Salad with Chickpeas (page 38)!

Breakfasts

Breakfast isn't just "the most important meal of the day," like Mom always said; it's often the most satisfying, too. The breakfast recipes in this section also happen to be extremely wholesome, healthy, and nutritious since they are free from wheat, meat, dairy, and refined sugar. I like to rely on superfoods like quinoa, oats, avocado, kale, and beans to start every day with a boost of sustainable energy. I have always been the type who enjoys breakfast for breakfast, but also for lunch and dinner, too! The Pomodoro Baked Eggs with Parmesan and Basil (page 187), for example, would be appropriate for any meal of the day. If you are particularly fond of any single breakfast recipe, go ahead and repeat it as often as you'd like. I try and have some overnight oats going in the fridge at all times for those hectic mornings when I need to grab and go. When it comes to juices, I often double or triple the recipes so that I can grab one for an afternoon pick-me-up or a speedy, no-fuss breakfast the following day. All of these recipes are built for one person, because I think it's always easier to scale up a recipe than to reduce it.

APPLE, KALE, AND GINGER JUICE

SERVES 1

2 cups roughly chopped kale leaves and tender stems

1 cup fresh flat-leaf parsley leaves and tender stems

2-inch piece fresh ginger, washed and sliced

1 green apple, diced

1 lemon, peeled and seeds removed

1½ cups filtered water or coconut water

In a blender, combine all of the ingredients and process until smooth. Drink immediately or store in the fridge for up to 2 days. If making ahead, shake to recombine before drinking.

BAKED TOMATOES WITH EGGS

SERVES 1

1 large beefsteak tomato

¼ teaspoon red pepper flakes

Kosher salt and freshly ground black pepper

2 tablespoons extra-virgin olive oil

2 tablespoons Faux Parmesan Cheese (page 248)

2 tablespoons distilled white vinegar

2 large eggs

4 fresh basil leaves, torn

1 Preheat the oven to 425°F.

2 Slice off the top and bottom of the tomato and discard (or reserve for another use). Cut the tomato horizontally in half to form 2 thick, round slices. Place the tomatoes on a sheet pan, sprinkle with the pepper flakes, and season with a pinch of salt and a twist of pepper. Drizzle 1 tablespoon of the olive oil over both tomato halves followed by 1 tablespoon of the faux parmesan. Bake until the faux parmesan is golden brown and the tomatoes are heated through, about 8 minutes.

3 Meanwhile, in a medium saucepan, combine 4 cups water and the vinegar and bring to a strong simmer over medium-high heat. Crack each egg into its own little bowl. With a spoon, create a large (but gentle) whirlpool in the simmering water by stirring in one direction around the perimeter of the pan. Gently lower the eggs one at a time into the center of the pan. Poach, untouched, until the eggs are set enough to be lifted out of the water without breaking but the yolks are still runny, about 3 minutes. Gently lift the eggs out of the water with a slotted spoon and transfer to a paper towel to remove excess water.

4 Transfer the baked tomatoes to plates, top each with a poached egg, and garnish with basil. Drizzle on the remaining 1 tablespoon olive oil and top with the remaining 1 tablespoon faux parmesan.

MUSHROOM QUINOA OMELET

SERVES 1

2 tablespoons extra-virgin olive oil

½ cup thinly sliced cremini mushrooms

1 teaspoon finely chopped fresh rosemary

¼ cup cooked Quinoa (page 245)

Kosher salt and freshly ground black pepper

3 large eggs

1 Set a large nonstick skillet over medium-high heat. Add 1 tablespoon of the olive oil and heat to shimmering, then add the mushrooms and rosemary. Cook, without stirring, until they begin to brown and crisp on one side, about 3 minutes. Add the quinoa and cook until crisp, about 2 minutes. Season with a pinch of salt and a twist of pepper. Transfer the mushroom mixture to a plate and set aside.

2 Wipe out the skillet, set over medium-low heat, and add the remaining 1 tablespoon olive oil. Crack the eggs into a medium bowl and whisk until they are thoroughly blended so that no strands hang from the whisk when lifted. Season with a pinch of salt and a twist of pepper and add to the skillet. Gently scramble the eggs in the skillet for 30 seconds, creating small curds of cooked egg. Shake the skillet to spread the eggs across the skillet. Evenly distribute the mushroom mixture on top, cover, remove from the heat, and let sit for 5 minutes.

3 Tilt the skillet and gently fold the omelet into thirds. Turn out onto a plate and serve.

OVERNIGHT QUINOA "OATMEAL"
WITH BLUEBERRIES AND WALNUTS

SERVES 1

¼ cup nuts
(I use walnut halves)

1 cup cooked Quinoa
(page 245)

1 cup unsweetened
almond milk

4 tablespoons chia seeds

2 tablespoons pure
maple syrup

¼ teaspoon ground
cinnamon

¼ cup fruit
(I use blueberries)

1 Preheat the oven to 350°F.

2 Arrange the walnuts on a sheet pan and cook until lightly toasted, about 8 minutes. Transfer the walnuts to a cutting board and when cool enough to handle, roughly chop and set aside.

3 In a 16-ounce mason jar or sealable container, combine the quinoa, almond milk, chia seeds, maple syrup, cinnamon, and walnuts. Stir to mix and refrigerate overnight.

4 Serve topped with the blueberries.

OVERNIGHT OATS
WITH CHIA, STRAWBERRY, AND BANANA

SERVES 1

1 small banana

1 cup coconut water

1 cup old-fashioned rolled oats

2 tablespoons chia seeds

¼ cup unsweetened toasted coconut flakes

3 strawberries, hulled and quartered

1 In a blender, combine the banana and coconut water and process until smooth.

2 In a 16-ounce mason jar or sealable container, combine the oats, chia seeds, and coconut flakes. Add the banana/coconut water mixture, stir to combine, and refrigerate overnight.

3 Serve topped with strawberries.

SUNNY-SIDE UP EGGS
WITH BLACK BEAN AND TOMATO SALSA

SERVES 1

¼ cup diced tomatoes

½ cup canned black beans (about one-quarter of a 15-ounce can), drained and rinsed

1 scallion, thinly sliced

2 tablespoons finely chopped fresh cilantro

Juice of ½ lime

½ teaspoon grated fresh turmeric or ¼ teaspoon ground turmeric

¼ teaspoon cayenne pepper (optional)

2 tablespoons extra-virgin olive oil

Kosher salt and freshly ground black pepper

3 large eggs

1 In a medium bowl, combine the tomatoes, black beans, scallion, cilantro, lime juice, turmeric, cayenne (if using), and 1 tablespoon of the olive oil. Season with a pinch of salt and a twist of pepper and toss to combine.

2 Set a large nonstick skillet over medium heat. Add the remaining 1 tablespoon olive oil and heat to shimmering. Carefully crack the eggs into the pan and cook until the whites begin to brown around the edges, about 2 minutes. Season with a pinch of salt and a twist of pepper. Remove from the heat, add 1 tablespoon water, cover, and let steam for 30 seconds for runny yolks, 1 minute for medium-set yolks, and 1½ minutes for fully set yolks.

3 Serve the eggs with the black bean and tomato salsa.

FRIED EGGS WITH AVOCADO AND TOMATO SALSA

SERVES 1

½ avocado, diced

¼ cup diced tomato

1 scallion, thinly sliced

1 tablespoon finely chopped fresh cilantro

½ teaspoon red pepper flakes

Juice of ½ lime

Kosher salt and freshly ground black pepper

1 tablespoon extra-virgin olive oil

3 large eggs

1 In a medium bowl, combine the avocado, tomato, scallion, cilantro, pepper flakes, and lime juice. Season with a pinch of salt and a twist of pepper and toss to combine.

2 Set a large nonstick skillet over medium heat. Add the oil and heat to shimmering. Carefully crack the eggs into the pan and cook until the whites begin to brown around the edges, about 2 minutes. Season with a pinch of salt and a twist of pepper. Remove from the heat, add 1 tablespoon water, cover, and let steam for 30 seconds for runny yolks, 1 minute for medium-set yolks, and 1½ minutes for fully set yolks.

3 Transfer the eggs to a plate, top with the avocado-tomato salsa, and serve.

SOFT SCRAMBLED EGGS
WITH KALE AND CRISPY QUINOA

SERVES 1

3 tablespoons extra-virgin olive oil

¼ teaspoon grated fresh ginger

1 cup cooked Quinoa (page 245)

½ cup roughly chopped kale leaves and tender stems

Kosher salt and freshly ground black pepper

3 large eggs

2 tablespoons coconut water

1 Set a large nonstick skillet over medium-high heat. Add 2 tablespoons of the olive oil and heat to shimmering. Add the ginger and cook until fragrant, about 15 seconds. Add the quinoa and shake the skillet to spread it out into an even layer. Cook, without stirring, until the bottom gets crispy, about 3 minutes.

2 Flip the quinoa and continue cooking until the other side gets crispy, about 3 minutes. Add the kale, season with a pinch of salt and a twist of pepper, stir to combine, and cook for 1 minute. Transfer to a plate and set aside.

3 In a medium bowl, whisk together the eggs and coconut water to thoroughly blend. Wipe out the skillet, set it over medium-high heat, and add the remaining 1 tablespoon olive oil, immediately add eggs and begin stirring. Season the eggs with a pinch of salt and a twist of pepper. Cook, stirring constantly, until small, soft curds form, about 2 minutes.

4 Serve the scrambled eggs on top of the crispy quinoa.

PINEAPPLE, AVOCADO, AND TURMERIC SMOOTHIE

SERVES 1

1 cup fresh or frozen diced pineapple

½ avocado, diced

1 cup coconut water

1 tablespoon grated fresh turmeric or 1 teaspoon ground turmeric

1 tablespoon grated fresh ginger

Juice of 1 lemon

1 cup ice

In a blender, combine all of the ingredients and process until smooth. Drink immediately or store in the fridge for up to 2 days.

BLUEBERRY, BANANA, AND SPINACH SMOOTHIE

SERVES 1

1 small banana

2 cups packed spinach leaves

1 cup fresh or frozen blueberries

1 cup unsweetened almond milk

¼ cup walnut halves

¼ teaspoon ground cinnamon

⅛ teaspoon cayenne pepper

In a blender, combine all of the ingredients and process until smooth. Drink immediately or store in the fridge for up to 2 days.

PINEAPPLE, AVOCADO, AND TURMERIC SMOOTHIE

BLUEBERRY, BANANA, AND SPINACH SMOOTHIE

APPLE, KALE, AND GINGER JUICE

PAGE 15

Lunches

These bright, flavorful, and trigger-free lunches can be enjoyed not only during the Reset but as often as you'd like. I managed to pack a good bit of protein into these recipes in the form of leafy greens, fluffy quinoa, and fatty fish like tuna. Many of these dishes would be as appropriate at dinnertime as they would at midday, so feel free to shuffle them around if you'd like. If you want to repeat a lunch—tuna salad, I'm looking at you!—go for it. Also, once you've finished the Reset and determined what your triggers are, you can transform many of the versatile salad recipes in this chapter into a heavier meal with the addition of grilled seafood or meat (assuming meat isn't your trigger).

QUINOA AND VEGETABLE SALAD

SERVES 1

1 tablespoon red wine vinegar

2 tablespoons extra-virgin olive oil

Kosher salt and freshly ground black pepper

½ cup cooked Quinoa (page 245)

1 small tomato, diced

½ small zucchini, diced

½ red bell pepper, diced

2 tablespoons finely chopped fresh flat-leaf parsley

In a medium bowl, whisk together the vinegar and olive oil. Season with a pinch of salt and a twist of pepper. Add the quinoa, tomato, zucchini, bell pepper, and parsley. Toss to combine and serve.

KALE SALAD
WITH DRIED CHERRIES AND WALNUTS

SERVES 1

¼ cup walnuts

1 tablespoon red wine vinegar

2 tablespoons extra-virgin olive oil

Kosher salt and freshly ground black pepper

2 cups thinly sliced kale leaves and tender stems

¼ cup dried cherries

½ cup cooked Quinoa (page 245)

1 tablespoon Faux Parmesan Cheese (page 248)

1 Preheat the oven to 350°F.

2 Arrange the walnuts on a sheet pan and cook until lightly toasted, about 8 minutes. Transfer the walnuts to a cutting board and when cool enough to handle, roughly chop and set aside.

3 In a small bowl, whisk together the vinegar and olive oil. Season with a pinch of salt and a twist of pepper. Add the walnuts, kale, cherries, and quinoa and toss to combine. Taste and adjust for seasoning, adding salt and pepper as needed.

4 Serve topped with faux parmesan.

OATMEAL RISOTTO

SERVES 1

2 tablespoons extra-virgin olive oil

1 cup sliced cremini mushrooms

1 small yellow onion, diced

1 garlic clove, minced

1 tablespoon finely chopped fresh rosemary

Kosher salt and freshly ground black pepper

1 cup old-fashioned rolled oats

2 cups Mushroom Broth (page 249)

2 cups packed spinach leaves

¼ cup Faux Parmesan Cheese (page 248)

2 teaspoons red wine vinegar

1 Set a large heavy-bottomed skillet over medium heat. Add the olive oil and heat to shimmering, then add the mushrooms and cook, without stirring, until they begin to brown and crisp on one side, about 3 minutes.

2 Add the onion, garlic, rosemary, and a pinch of salt and cook, stirring occasionally, until the vegetables are aromatic and soft, about 3 minutes.

3 Add the oats and cook, stirring occasionally, until toasted, about 45 seconds. Add the mushroom broth, season with a pinch of salt and a twist of pepper, and cook, stirring frequently, until all of the liquid is absorbed and the oats are cooked through, about 8 minutes.

4 Remove from the heat, stir in the spinach, faux parmesan, and vinegar and serve.

SAVORY OATMEAL
WITH TURMERIC-POACHED EGG

SERVES 1

2 tablespoons distilled white vinegar

2 teaspoons ground turmeric

1 tablespoon extra-virgin olive oil

½ small zucchini, diced

2 scallions, thinly sliced

Kosher salt and freshly ground black pepper

½ cup old-fashioned rolled oats

2 teaspoons tomato paste

1 cup sliced spinach leaves

1 large egg

1 In a medium saucepan, combine 4 cups water, the vinegar, and turmeric and bring to a strong simmer over medium-high heat.

2 Meanwhile, in a separate medium saucepan, heat the olive oil over medium heat to shimmering. Add the zucchini, scallions, and a pinch of salt. Cook until the vegetables begin to soften, about 1 minute. Add the oats and tomato paste and cook, stirring, for 1 minute. Season with a pinch of salt and a twist of pepper. Add 1 cup water, bring to a simmer, and cook, uncovered, until the oats are tender, about 5 minutes. Remove from the heat, add the spinach, and stir to combine. Cover to keep warm while you poach the egg.

3 Crack the egg into a little bowl. With a spoon, create a large (but gentle) whirlpool in the simmering water by stirring in one direction around the perimeter of the pan. Gently lower the egg into the center of the pan. Poach, untouched, until the egg is set enough to be lifted out of the water without breaking but the yolk is still runny, about 3 minutes. Gently lift the egg out of the water with a slotted spoon.

4 Transfer the oatmeal to a bowl, top with the poached egg, and serve.

SPINACH SALAD
WITH SHAVED BEETS AND APPLES

SERVES 1

¼ cup sliced or slivered almonds

1½ tablespoons raw apple cider vinegar

1 teaspoon raw honey

1 teaspoon Dijon mustard

2 tablespoons extra-virgin olive oil

Kosher salt and freshly ground black pepper

2 cups packed spinach leaves

1 small red or yellow beet, peeled and sliced ⅛ inch thick

½ unpeeled Granny Smith apple, cut into matchsticks

1 Preheat the oven to 350°F.

2 Arrange the almonds on a sheet pan and cook until lightly toasted, about 8 minutes. Set aside.

3 In a medium bowl, whisk together the vinegar, honey, and mustard. While continuously whisking, slowly add the olive oil in a steady stream. Season with a pinch of salt and a twist of pepper. Add the spinach, beet, apple, and almonds and toss to combine.

TUNA SALAD WITH CHICKPEAS

SERVES 1

1 (6-ounce) jar tuna packed in olive oil, plus 1 tablespoon of oil from the jar

1 (15-ounce) can chickpeas, drained and rinsed

½ red bell pepper, diced

3 scallions, thinly sliced

¼ cup finely chopped fresh flat-leaf parsley

Grated zest and juice of 1 lemon

Kosher salt and freshly ground black pepper

2 hearts of romaine lettuce, leaves separated

1 In a medium bowl, break up the tuna into small chunks with a fork. Add the reserved tuna oil, the chickpeas, bell pepper, scallions, parsley, lemon zest, and lemon juice. Season with a pinch of salt and a twist of pepper and toss to combine.

2 Serve the tuna salad in the romaine leaves.

QUICK VEGGIE SOUP

SERVES 1

1 (15-ounce) can cannellini beans, drained and rinsed

1 cup sliced spinach leaves

1 cup Mushroom Broth (page 249)

¼ cup cooked Quinoa (page 245)

1 teaspoon tamari (wheat-free soy sauce)

½ teaspoon red pepper flakes

Juice of 1 lime

Kosher salt and freshly ground black pepper

In a medium saucepan, combine the beans, spinach, mushroom broth, quinoa, tamari, pepper flakes, and lime juice. Season with a pinch of salt and a twist of pepper. Bring to a strong simmer over medium heat and serve.

CRISPY BROWN RICE AND CAULIFLOWER WITH FRIED EGGS

SERVES 1

¼ small head cauliflower, broken into florets

3 tablespoons extra-virgin olive oil

½ cup cooked Brown Rice (page 246)

1 teaspoon grated fresh turmeric or ⅓ teaspoon ground turmeric

¼ teaspoon cayenne pepper

1 garlic clove, grated

1 teaspoon grated fresh ginger

Kosher salt and freshly ground black pepper

2 scallions, thinly sliced

2 large eggs

1 tablespoon finely chopped fresh cilantro

Lime wedge, for serving

Hot sauce, for serving

1 In a blender or food processor, pulse the cauliflower until the mixture has the consistency of rice.

2 Set a large heavy-bottomed skillet over medium-high heat. Add 2 tablespoons of the olive oil and heat to shimmering. Add the brown rice, cauliflower rice, turmeric, and cayenne and stir to combine, then shake the skillet to spread the mixture out into an even layer. Cook, without stirring, until the bottom gets crispy, about 3 minutes. Sprinkle the garlic and ginger across the top and season with a pinch of salt and a twist of pepper. Remove from the heat, stir in the scallions, and set aside.

3 Set a large nonstick skillet over medium heat. Add the remaining 1 tablespoon olive oil and heat to shimmering. Carefully crack the eggs into the pan and cook until the whites begin to brown around the edges, about 2 minutes. Add the cilantro and season with a pinch of salt and a twist of pepper. Remove from the heat, add 1 tablespoon water, cover, and let steam for 30 seconds for runny yolks, 1 minute for medium-set yolks, and 1½ minutes for fully set yolks.

4 Place the brown rice and cauliflower on a plate, top with the eggs, and serve with a lime wedge and hot sauce.

BAKED SWEET POTATO
WITH KALE AND WALNUT PESTO

SERVES 1

1 cup walnuts

1 large sweet potato

2 cups roughly chopped kale leaves and tender stems

1 garlic clove, sliced

¾ cup Faux Parmesan Cheese (page 248)

1 cup extra-virgin olive oil

Kosher salt and freshly ground black pepper

1 Preheat the oven to 350°F.

2 Arrange the walnuts on a sheet pan and cook until lightly toasted, about 8 minutes. Transfer the walnuts to a cutting board and when cool enough to handle, roughly chop and set aside.

3 Increase the oven temperature to 425°F. Line a sheet pan with foil.

4 Pierce the sweet potato with a fork or paring knife a few times and roast on the lined pan until it is easily pierced with a knife, about 1 hour.

5 In a blender or food processor, pulse the kale, garlic, and walnuts until the mixture has the consistency of fine crumbs. Add the faux parmesan. With the machine running, slowly add the olive oil in a steady stream. Transfer to a bowl and season with a pinch of salt and a twist of pepper.

6 Slice the sweet potato down the middle to open, top with pesto to taste, and serve. Reserve any remaining pesto for other uses. Store it in the fridge for up to 1 week.

TOMATO AND COCONUT SOUP

SERVES 1

2 tablespoons extra-virgin olive oil

1 small yellow onion, diced

2 garlic cloves, sliced

1-inch piece fresh ginger, peeled and thinly sliced

Kosher salt and freshly ground black pepper

½ teaspoon red pepper flakes

1 (15-ounce) can crushed San Marzano tomatoes

¾ cup unsweetened full-fat coconut milk

¼ cup Faux Parmesan Cheese (page 248)

1 tablespoon finely chopped fresh cilantro

1 Set a medium saucepan over medium heat. Add the olive oil and heat to shimmering, then add the onion, garlic, ginger, and a pinch of salt. Cook until the vegetables are aromatic and soft, about 5 minutes. Add the pepper flakes and cook, stirring constantly, for 30 seconds. Add the tomatoes and coconut milk, season with a pinch of salt and a twist of pepper, and bring to a simmer. Cover and cook, stirring occasionally, for 15 minutes.

2 Remove from the heat, transfer to a blender or food processor, add the faux parmesan, and process until smooth. Serve topped with cilantro.

Dinners

I think you'll find enough deliciousness in these dishes to add them to your regular weeknight repertoire long after the initial 10-day process. They are all extremely nutritious, made with whole foods that are rich in vitamins, minerals, fiber, and anti-inflammatory compounds. I like my weeknight dinners to be slightly heartier, but still simple enough to prepare quickly. Many of these already have become favorites in the Symon household. We keep returning to the Grilled Salmon with Celery and Apple Salad (page 55) and the Root Vegetable and Black Bean Stew (page 57). I hope you discover some new favorites in here as well.

PUFFY OMELET WITH HERBS

SERVES 1

3 large eggs, separated

Kosher salt and freshly ground black pepper

2 tablespoons sparkling water

2 tablespoons Faux Parmesan Cheese (page 248)

1 tablespoon extra-virgin olive oil

2 tablespoons thinly sliced chives

2 tablespoons finely chopped fresh flat-leaf parsley

1 In a stand mixer fitted with the whisk, beat the egg whites and 1 tablespoon water to stiff peaks.

2 In a large bowl, beat the egg yolks, a pinch of salt, and a twist of pepper until smooth, thick, and slightly pale in color. Gently fold one-third of the beaten egg whites into the egg yolks until no white streaks remain. Stir in the sparkling water. Add this mixture to the egg whites along with 1 tablespoon of the faux parmesan and gently fold to combine.

3 Set a large nonstick skillet over medium heat. Add the olive oil and heat to shimmering, then add the eggs and gently smooth the top with a spatula. Cover and cook until golden brown on the bottom and the edges lift cleanly from the skillet, about 5 minutes. Sprinkle the remaining 1 tablespoon faux parmesan on top. Remove from the heat and top with herbs.

4 Tilt the skillet and gently fold the omelet in half, turn out onto a plate, and serve.

SLOW-ROASTED SALMON
WITH BEETS AND AVOCADO

SERVES 1

¼ cup sliced or slivered almonds

1 (6- to 8-ounce) skinless salmon fillet, pin bones removed

3 teaspoons Dijon mustard

Kosher salt and freshly ground black pepper

1 tablespoon red wine vinegar

2 teaspoons grated fresh or prepared horseradish

2 tablespoons extra-virgin olive oil

1 cup thinly sliced spinach leaves

1 small red or yellow beet, peeled and cut into matchsticks

½ avocado, diced

1 Preheat the oven to 350°F.

2 Arrange the almonds on a sheet pan and cook until lightly toasted, about 8 minutes. Set aside.

3 Reduce the oven temperature to 275°F. Line a sheet pan with foil.

4 Using paper towels, pat the fish dry. Evenly coat the salmon on all sides with 2 teaspoons of the mustard. Season the fillet on all sides with salt and pepper. Place the fish on the lined sheet pan and bake until the fish reaches an internal temperature of 130°F, about 20 minutes. If you prefer a flakier fish, cook for another 10 minutes.

5 In a small bowl, whisk together the vinegar, horseradish, and remaining 1 teaspoon mustard. While continuously whisking, slowly add the olive oil in a steady stream. Season with a pinch of salt and a twist of pepper. Add the spinach, beet, avocado, and almonds and toss to combine.

6 Transfer the salad to a plate, top with salmon, and serve.

ROASTED PORTOBELLO MUSHROOM WITH CAULIFLOWER MASH

SERVES 1

5 tablespoons extra-virgin olive oil

2 teaspoons finely chopped rosemary

1 large portobello mushroom, stem discarded and gills scraped out

Kosher salt and freshly ground black pepper

¼ small head cauliflower, roughly chopped (about 2 cups)

3 tablespoons Faux Parmesan Cheese (page 248)

2 tablespoons Kale and Walnut Pesto (page 248)

1 Preheat the oven to 450°F.

2 In a small bowl, whisk together 2 tablespoons of the olive oil and the rosemary. Add the mushroom cap and flip to coat both sides in the marinade. Season both sides with salt and pepper.

3 Line a sheet pan with foil. Place the mushroom gill-side down on the pan and roast for 10 minutes. Flip and continue roasting until softened and golden brown, about 5 minutes.

4 Meanwhile, set a large heavy-bottomed skillet over medium-high heat. Add 2 tablespoons of the olive oil and heat to shimmering, then add the cauliflower and a pinch of salt. Cook until the cauliflower begins to soften and brown, about 5 minutes. Add 1 cup water and bring to a simmer. Cook, partially covered, until the cauliflower is fully cooked through and the liquid has reduced by two-thirds, about 8 minutes.

5 Transfer the cauliflower to a blender or food processor. Add the remaining 1 tablespoon olive oil and the faux parmesan and process until completely smooth. Taste and adjust for seasoning, adding salt and pepper as needed.

6 To serve, spread the cauliflower mash on a plate. Slice the mushroom, place it on the cauliflower, and top with pesto.

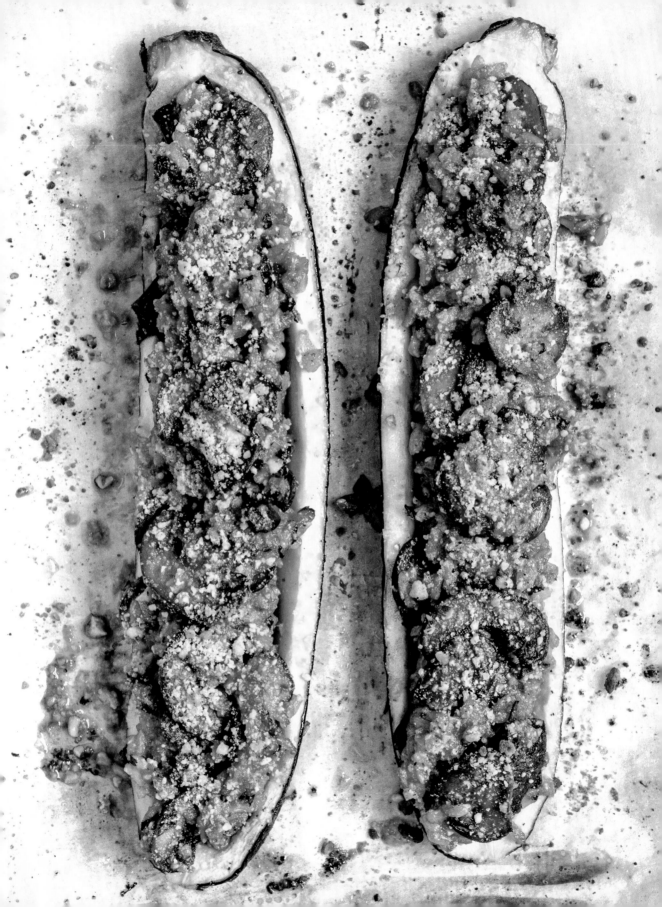

MUSHROOM AND BROWN RICE-STUFFED ZUCCHINI

SERVES 1

1 medium zucchini, halved lengthwise, seeds scooped out with a spoon to form a shallow trough

3 tablespoons extra-virgin olive oil

Kosher salt and freshly ground black pepper

1 cup sliced cremini mushrooms

1 garlic clove, minced

1 cup cooked Brown Rice (page 246)

1 cup Mushroom Broth (page 249)

¼ cup plus 1 tablespoon Faux Parmesan Cheese (page 248)

¼ cup finely chopped fresh flat-leaf parsley

1 Preheat the oven to 450°F. Line a sheet pan with foil.

2 Place the zucchini on the lined sheet pan, drizzle both sides with 1 tablespoon of the olive oil, and season with a pinch of salt and a twist of pepper. Bake cut-side down for 5 minutes. Remove from the oven and flip the zucchini cut-side up. Leave the oven on.

3 Set a large heavy-bottomed skillet over medium heat. Add the remaining 2 tablespoons olive oil and heat to shimmering, then add the mushrooms and cook, without stirring, until they begin to brown and crisp on one side, about 3 minutes. Season with a pinch of salt and a twist of pepper. Add the garlic and brown rice and cook, stirring occasionally, until aromatic, about 2 minutes. Add the mushroom broth and bring to a simmer. Cook, uncovered, until the flavors meld and most of the liquid has evaporated, about 5 minutes. Remove from the heat, add ¼ cup of the faux parmesan and the parsley, and stir to combine.

4 Divide the mushroom and rice mixture equally between the zucchini halves. Top with the remaining 1 tablespoon faux parmesan and bake uncovered until the zucchini and the filling are cooked through, about 10 minutes. Serve hot.

QUINOA FRIED "RICE"

SERVES 1

3 tablespoons extra-virgin olive oil

½ small yellow onion, diced

½ cup sliced cremini mushrooms or diced portobello

½ small zucchini, diced

½ red bell pepper, diced

1 garlic clove, minced

1 teaspoon grated fresh ginger

1 cup cooked Quinoa (page 245)

1 large egg

2 tablespoons tamari (wheat-free soy sauce)

Lime wedge

1 Set a large nonstick skillet over medium heat. Add the olive oil and heat to shimmering, then add the onion, mushrooms, zucchini, and bell pepper and cook until the vegetables begin to soften and brown, about 5 minutes. Add the garlic, ginger, and quinoa. Stir and cook until the quinoa is crispy, about 5 minutes.

2 Meanwhile, in a small bowl, whisk together the egg and tamari.

3 When the quinoa is crispy, move it to the outer edge of the pan to clear a space in the middle. To this open space add the egg mixture. Gently scramble the egg in the skillet for 30 seconds, creating small curds of cooked egg. When the egg is cooked, mix in the vegetables.

4 Transfer the fried quinoa to a plate, squeeze the lime on top, and serve.

TIP: This is a good way to use up partial vegetables you may have from doing the Reset. This is a highly customizable recipe with vegetable substitutions—just dice everything the same size.

GRILLED SALMON
WITH CELERY AND APPLE SALAD

SERVES 1

1 (6- to 8-ounce) skinless salmon fillet, pin bones removed

3 tablespoons extra-virgin olive oil

Kosher salt and freshly ground black pepper

1 tablespoon raw apple cider vinegar

1 teaspoon Dijon mustard

1 teaspoon grated fresh ginger

½ unpeeled green apple, cut into matchsticks

2 celery ribs, thinly sliced on an angle, any leaves reserved

1 Preheat a grill or grill pan to medium-high heat.

2 Drizzle the fish with 1 tablespoon of the olive oil and season with a few pinches of salt and twists of pepper. Put the fish on the grill and cook, without moving, until nicely browned and the fish releases from the grill, about 3 minutes. Flip and continue cooking for 3 minutes.

3 In a small bowl, whisk together the vinegar, mustard, ginger, and remaining 2 tablespoons olive oil. Season with a pinch of salt and a twist of pepper. Add the apple, celery, and celery leaves (if you have them) and toss to combine.

4 Transfer the salad to a plate and serve alongside the salmon.

ROOT VEGETABLE AND BLACK BEAN STEW

SERVES 1

¼ cup sliced or slivered almonds

2 tablespoons extra-virgin olive oil

1 small yellow onion, diced

1 jalapeño, seeded and finely chopped

Kosher salt

1 medium parsnip, peeled and sliced

1 medium carrot, peeled and sliced

½ teaspoon ground cumin

2 teaspoons tomato paste

1 (15-ounce) can black beans, drained and rinsed

1 cup Mushroom Broth (page 249)

¼ cup unsweetened full-fat coconut milk

Freshly ground black pepper

2 tablespoons finely chopped fresh cilantro

Juice of ½ lime

½ cup cooked Brown Rice (optional; page 246), warmed

1 Preheat the oven to 350°F.

2 Arrange the almonds on a sheet pan and cook until lightly toasted, about 8 minutes. Set aside.

3 Set a large saucepan over medium heat. Add the olive oil and heat to shimmering, then add the onion, jalapeño, and a pinch of salt. Cook until the vegetables are aromatic and soft, about 3 minutes. Add the parsnips and carrots and cook, stirring occasionally, until the vegetables begin to brown, about 3 minutes. Add the cumin and cook for 30 seconds. Add the tomato paste and cook, stirring occasionally, until the paste begins to darken, about 1 minute. Add the black beans, mushroom broth, and coconut milk and season with a few pinches of salt and twists of pepper. Cook, partially covered, until the vegetables are fully cooked and the stew has thickened, about 20 minutes.

4 Remove from the heat, stir in the cilantro, almonds, and lime juice, and serve as is or over warm brown rice.

ZUCCHINI PANCAKE
WITH TOMATO SALAD

SERVES 1

1 medium zucchini, grated on the large holes of a box grater

1 garlic clove, minced

1 tablespoon finely chopped fresh mint

1 tablespoon finely chopped fresh dill

1 scallion, thinly sliced

Grated zest and juice of ½ lemon

1 large egg, beaten

Kosher salt and freshly ground black pepper

2 tablespoons extra-virgin olive oil

1 beefsteak tomato, diced

1 Place the grated zucchini in a kitchen towel and wring out as much water as possible. Transfer the zucchini to a medium bowl. Add the garlic, mint, dill, scallion, lemon zest, and egg. Season with a pinch of salt and a twist of pepper and toss to combine.

2 Set a large nonstick skillet over medium-high heat. Add 1 tablespoon of the olive oil and heat to shimmering, then add the zucchini batter and smooth it out to an even layer with a spatula. Cook, without disturbing, until the bottom turns golden brown, about 5 minutes. Flip and continue cooking until the other side browns, about 3 minutes.

3 Meanwhile, in a medium bowl, combine the tomato, lemon juice, and remaining 1 tablespoon olive oil. Season with a pinch of salt and a twist of pepper and toss to combine.

4 Transfer the zucchini pancake to a plate, top with the tomato salad, and serve.

ZUCCHINI NOODLES
WITH TUNA AND MINT

SERVES 1

2 medium zucchini
or 3 cups spiralized
zucchini

Kosher salt and freshly
ground black pepper

2 tablespoons extra-
virgin olive oil

2 garlic cloves, sliced

½ teaspoon red pepper
flakes

1 cup halved cherry
tomatoes

1 (6-ounce) jar tuna
packed in olive oil, plus
1 tablespoon of oil from
the jar

½ cup fresh mint leaves,
torn

1 Use a vegetable spiralizer or julienne peeler to cut the zucchini into long noodles. If you don't have either of those kitchen tools, cut the zucchini lengthwise into ⅛-inch-thick slices and then cut the slices lengthwise into thin, long strands.

2 Add 2 tablespoons salt to a medium pot of water and bring to a boil over high heat.

3 Meanwhile, set a large heavy-bottomed skillet over low heat. Add the olive oil followed by the garlic and pepper flakes and cook until aromatic, about 2 minutes. Add the tomatoes, season with a pinch of salt, and continue cooking until the tomatoes soften and begin to break down, about 3 minutes. Add the tuna and reserved tuna oil to warm while the zucchini cooks.

4 Add the zucchini noodles to the boiling water and cook for 1 minute. Scoop out and reserve ¼ cup of the water before draining. Drain the zucchini noodles and add them to the pan. Season with a pinch of salt and a twist of pepper and gently toss to combine. Add the reserved cooking water.

5 Remove from the heat, stir in the mint, and serve.

CAULIFLOWER SOUP
WITH MUSHROOM AND KALE

SERVES 1

4 tablespoons extra-virgin olive oil

¼ small head cauliflower, roughly chopped

Kosher salt and freshly ground black pepper

2 scallions, thinly sliced

1 garlic clove, sliced

1 jalapeño, seeded and sliced

¼ cup raw cashews

¼ cup nutritional yeast

1 tablespoon fresh lemon juice

½ cup sliced cremini mushrooms

1 cup sliced kale leaves and tender stems

1 tablespoon Faux Parmesan Cheese (page 248)

1 Set a medium saucepan over medium-high heat. Add 2 tablespoons of the olive oil and heat to shimmering, then add the cauliflower and a pinch of salt. Cook until the cauliflower begins to soften and brown, about 5 minutes. Add the scallions, garlic, jalapeño, and cashews and season with a pinch of salt and a twist of pepper. Cook until the vegetables are aromatic, about 2 minutes. Add 1 cup water, bring to a simmer, and cook until the vegetables are tender and the liquid has reduced, about 5 minutes. Remove from the heat and stir in the nutritional yeast.

2 Carefully transfer the soup to a blender or food processer and process until smooth. Return the soup to the saucepan, add the lemon juice, and keep warm over low heat.

3 Set a large heavy-bottomed skillet over medium-high heat. Add the remaining 2 tablespoons olive oil and heat to shimmering, then add the mushrooms and cook, without stirring, until they begin to brown and crisp on one side, about 3 minutes. Shake the pan to turn the mushrooms, add the kale, and season with a pinch of salt and a twist of pepper. Cook for 1 minute.

4 Ladle the soup into a bowl, top with mushrooms and kale, garnish with faux parmesan, and serve.

HOW TO REINTRODUCE

Reintroducing Dairy

Reintroducing Flour

Reintroducing Meat

Breakfast: Smoked Turkey and Sweet Potato Hash 76

Lunch: Chopped Salad with Turkey, Dried Cherries, and Walnuts with Poppy Seed Vinaigrette 78

Dinner: Brick Chicken with Salsa Verde *(as seen above)* 80

Reintroducing Sugar

Breakfast: Brown Sugar Overnight Oats 84

Lunch: Flourless Nutella Crepes 85

Dinner: BBQ-Glazed Carrots with Almond-Cilantro Quinoa *(as seen above)* 88

One of the topics that generated lots of commentary following the publication of *Fix It with Food* was the process of reintroducing foods after the Reset. It's a crucial step in determining one's triggers, so we wanted to make sure we gave it the attention it deserves here.

The 10-Day Reset is designed to eliminate all inflammation triggers from your diet; the reintroduction phase is when we examine one potential trigger at a time to see how our bodies respond. By isolating each category (like dairy, flour, meat, or sugar) and then cooking and eating three meals with it included and monitoring how we feel the next day, we can determine if that food is in fact a trigger. Unlike in the Reset chapter or the later chapters for no dairy, no meat, no sugar, and no flour, these recipes and meal plans should be followed in order to keep the results accurate. The day after you reintroduce the food, pay special attention to how you feel. If those nasty aches, pains, and flair-ups rear their ugly heads, you'll know that the ingredient you cooked with the previous day is a trigger and should be avoided. When that happens, I like to go back to Reset recipes, which I know are trigger-free, for two days before moving onto another reintroduction day. Once you have cooked your way through all the reintroduction recipes, you will know what foods you can safely enjoy and which ones to stay away from.

Reintroducing Dairy

I don't need to "reintroduce dairy" into my diet because I know what would happen. Dairy is one of my personal triggers, causing inflammation and discomfort whenever I indulge. That's too bad because it's one of my favorite food groups! These recipes all contain dairy, but none of the other potential triggers, so you will know the next day, if you have a reaction, that dairy and not another trigger food was the culprit. That said, these still are "healthy" recipes that can be enjoyed throughout the year—assuming you don't have to avoid dairy.

BLUEBERRY-ALMOND YOGURT SMOOTHIE

SERVES 1

1 cup plain whole-milk Greek yogurt

1 small banana

½ cup fresh or frozen blueberries

½ cup raw sliced or slivered almonds

½ cup coconut water

½ cup ice

In a blender, combine all of the ingredients and process until smooth. Drink immediately or store in the fridge for up to 2 days.

TOMATO PARMESAN

SERVES 1

1 beefsteak tomato

½ teaspoon garlic powder

Kosher salt and freshly ground black pepper

1½ cups freshly grated parmesan cheese

1 large egg

2 tablespoons whole milk

¼ cup shredded fresh mozzarella cheese

1 teaspoon extra-virgin olive oil

1 teaspoon balsamic vinegar

½ cup torn fresh basil leaves

1 Slice off the top and bottom of the tomato and discard (or reserve for another use). Cut the tomato in half to form 2 thick, round slices. Season all sides with the garlic powder and a few pinches of salt and twists of pepper.

2 Put the parmesan in a shallow bowl. Put the egg and milk in another shallow bowl, season with a pinch of salt and a twist of pepper, and whisk to combine.

3 Working with one tomato slice at a time, dredge it in the parmesan, making sure to coat all sides well. Shake off the excess. Dip the tomato into the beaten egg, allowing the excess to drip off. Finally, lay the tomato back in the parmesan, turning to fully coat all sides.

4 Set a large nonstick skillet over medium-low heat. Add the tomatoes to the dry skillet and cook until the parmesan is golden brown and toasted, about 5 minutes. Flip and continue cooking for 2 minutes. Divide the mozzarella over the tomato slices, cover the pan, and continue cooking until the cheese is melted and the second side is golden brown, about 1 minute.

5 To serve, transfer the tomatoes to a plate, drizzle with the olive oil and vinegar, and top with the basil.

ZUCCHINI NOODLES
WITH CHEESY GARLIC-CREAM SAUCE

SERVES 1

2 medium zucchini or 3 cups spiralized zucchini

1 cup heavy cream

2 garlic cloves, peeled and smashed

½ teaspoon ground turmeric

¼ teaspoon freshly ground black pepper

1 tablespoon finely chopped fresh rosemary

Kosher salt

½ cup crumbled fresh goat cheese

¼ cup freshly grated parmesan cheese

1 Use a vegetable spiralizer or julienne peeler to cut the zucchini into long noodles. If you don't have either of those kitchen tools, cut the zucchini lengthwise into ⅛-inch-thick slices and then cut the slices lengthwise into thin, long strands.

2 Set a medium saucepan over medium heat. Add the cream and garlic and bring to a simmer. Add the turmeric, pepper, and rosemary and whisk to combine. Season with a pinch of salt and continue cooking, uncovered, until the cream is reduced by two-thirds and thickened, about 15 minutes. Add the goat cheese and whisk until the cheese is melted and the sauce is creamy and smooth, about 1 minute. Remove from the heat.

3 Add 2 tablespoons salt to a medium pot of water and bring to a boil over high heat. Add the zucchini noodles and cook for 1 minute. Drain the zucchini noodles and add them to the cheese sauce. Stir in the parmesan and serve.

Reintroducing Flour

Fortunately for me, flour is not one of my triggers. I don't know how I would survive without fresh-baked bread, al dente pasta, and fluffy donuts! (That said, I do find a way to get by even though I can't eat as much cheese or ice cream as I'd like, but hey, we all have our burdens to bear.) But even though flour isn't a trigger, I'm not always free from harm after eating some foods that feature flour. What I have discovered is that it is the quality and type of flour that makes all the difference in the world. Heavily processed flours that have been bleached and bromated affect me entirely differently from the freshly milled, organic stuff. Even I experience some wheat sensitivity issues after eating foods made with inferior commercial flours, so I suggest that you really scour ingredients lists and become your own expert and advocate for your health. Before you assume that flour might be getting the best of you, try baking with unbromated, unbleached, and unenriched products like King Arthur or fresh milled flour from your local farmers' market or specialty food store to see how they affect you. You might be pleasantly surprised by the results.

CORN PANCAKES
WITH MAPLE AND BLUEBERRIES

MAKES 4 (4-INCH) PANCAKES

2 tablespoons coconut oil

2 cups fresh or frozen corn kernels

Kosher salt

1 large egg

⅓ cup unsweetened almond milk

1 teaspoon vanilla extract

½ cup all-purpose flour

½ teaspoon baking powder

½ teaspoon baking soda

Pinch of ground cinnamon

1 cup fresh blueberries

Pure maple syrup, for serving

1 In a small saucepan, combine 1 tablespoon of the coconut oil, the corn, and a pinch of salt. Cook, partially covered, over medium heat until the corn has softened, about 10 minutes. Transfer to a blender or food processor and process until smooth.

2 In a medium bowl, whisk together the corn puree, egg, almond milk, and vanilla. In a separate bowl, whisk together the flour, baking powder, baking soda, and cinnamon. Add the dry ingredients to the wet ingredients and stir until a batter forms. Let stand for 5 minutes before cooking.

3 Set a large nonstick skillet over medium-low heat. Add ½ tablespoon of the coconut oil and heat until melted. Working two pancakes at a time, ladle ⅓ cup of batter for each pancake into the skillet. Cover and cook until bubbles appear on the surface and the bottoms begin to brown, about 2 minutes. Sprinkle a small handful of blueberries onto each pancake, flip, and continue cooking until the bottoms are golden brown, about 2 minutes. Transfer to a plate, cover, and keep warm while you repeat the process with the remaining ½ tablespoon coconut oil and batter.

4 Transfer the pancakes to a plate, top with maple syrup (and any remaining blueberries), and serve.

AVOCADO TOAST
WITH KALE AND WALNUT PESTO

SERVES 1

1 slice whole-grain bread

1 garlic clove, peeled

1 tablespoon Kale and Walnut Pesto (page 248)

¼ avocado, thinly sliced

Pinch of dried red pepper flakes

Flaky sea salt, for serving

Lime wedge, for serving

Toast the bread. While the bread is still warm from the toaster, rub the top with the garlic clove. Spread the pesto on the toast. Arrange the avocado slices in an even layer on the pesto and then lightly mash it into the bread with a fork. Sprinkle with pepper flakes and salt, squirt with fresh lime juice, and serve.

SPAGHETTI
WITH CORN AND BASIL

SERVES 1

Kosher salt and freshly ground black pepper

¼ pound spaghetti

2 tablespoons extra-virgin olive oil

1 cup halved cherry tomatoes

2 garlic cloves, sliced

Pinch red pepper flakes (optional)

1 cup fresh or frozen corn kernels

2 tablespoons Faux Parmesan Cheese (page 248)

8 basil leaves, torn

1 Add 3 tablespoons salt to a large pot of water and bring to a boil over high heat. Add the pasta and cook until just al dente, about 1 minute less than the package directions. Occasionally give the pasta a stir so it doesn't stick together.

2 Meanwhile, set a large heavy-bottomed skillet over medium-low heat. Add the olive oil and heat to shimmering, then add the tomatoes, garlic, and pepper flakes (if using). Season with a pinch of salt and a twist of pepper and cook until aromatic, about 5 minutes. Add the corn and cook for 3 minutes. Scoop out ½ cup of the pasta water, add it to the skillet, and bring to a simmer. Continue cooking until the pasta is ready.

3 Drain the pasta and add it to the skillet. Remove from the heat, stir in the faux parmesan and basil, and serve.

Reintroducing Meat

For obvious reasons, meat is an ingredient that I was terrified would land on my forbidden-foods list. I wrote a cookbook called *Carnivore*, I own burger and barbecue restaurants, and steak is my favorite vegetable! That said, the older (and wiser) I get, the less meat I tend to eat. My approach has always been to spend more on the best quality cuts I can find, but to do so less frequently and in smaller quantities. It used to be a challenge to track down responsibly raised animals that were fed well, given some room to roam, and processed humanely, but not anymore. I feel like it's never been easier to find a conscientious butcher who maintains relationships with small farms in the region. It's possible to order high-quality meats and even seafood to be delivered right to your front door. No, most of these products aren't "cheap," but they usually are worth every penny.

SMOKED TURKEY AND SWEET POTATO HASH

SERVES 1

3 tablespoons extra-virgin olive oil

1 small sweet potato, peeled and diced

¼ teaspoon ground turmeric

Kosher salt and freshly ground black pepper

1 cup strips of deli-style smoked turkey

½ red bell pepper, diced

2 scallions, thinly sliced

1 Set a large heavy-bottomed skillet over medium-high heat. Add the olive oil and heat to shimmering, then add the sweet potato, turmeric, and a pinch of salt and a twist of pepper. Cook until the potatoes turn golden brown and crisp, about 5 minutes.

2 Add the turkey and bell pepper and continue cooking until the turkey is lightly browned, about 2 minutes. Remove from the heat, stir in the scallions, and serve.

CHOPPED SALAD
WITH TURKEY, DRIED CHERRIES, AND WALNUTS WITH POPPY SEED VINAIGRETTE

SERVES 1

½ cup walnuts

2 tablespoons extra-virgin olive oil

1 tablespoon raw apple cider vinegar

1 teaspoon Dijon mustard

1 teaspoon poppy seeds

Kosher salt and freshly ground black pepper

1 romaine heart, halved lengthwise and cut crosswise into ½-inch strips

½ cup strips of deli-style smoked turkey

½ cup halved cherry tomatoes

2 scallions, thinly sliced

¼ cup dried cherries

1 Preheat the oven to 350°F.

2 Arrange the walnuts on a sheet pan and cook until lightly toasted, about 8 minutes. Transfer the walnuts to a cutting board and when cool enough to handle, roughly chop and set aside.

3 In a medium bowl, whisk together the olive oil, vinegar, mustard, and poppy seeds. Season with a pinch of salt and a twist of pepper. Add the romaine, turkey, tomatoes, scallions, walnuts, and cherries and toss to combine. Taste and adjust for seasoning, adding salt and pepper as needed, and serve.

BRICK CHICKEN WITH SALSA VERDE

SERVES 1

½ chicken (4 to 6 pounds)

Kosher salt and freshly ground black pepper

2 tablespoons extra-virgin olive oil

4 garlic cloves, skin-on and smashed

2 sprigs rosemary

1 beefsteak tomato, cut into 4 wedges

Salsa Verde

⅓ cup finely chopped fresh flat-leaf parsley

1 shallot, finely chopped

2 tablespoons salt-packed capers, rinsed and finely chopped

½ teaspoon red pepper flakes

2 anchovy fillets, rinsed and finely chopped

1 garlic clove, minced

1 jalapeño, seeded and finely chopped

Grated zest and juice of 1 lemon

½ cup extra-virgin olive oil

Kosher salt and freshly ground black pepper

1 Preheat the oven to 425°F. Wrap two regular bricks with aluminum foil. If you don't have any bricks, you can use a second heavy skillet as a weight.

2 Season the chicken on both sides with a few pinches of salt and twists of pepper.

3 Set a large cast-iron pan or heavy-bottomed ovenproof skillet over medium-high heat. Add the olive oil and heat to shimmering, then add the chicken, flesh-side down. Cook without moving until the bottom turns golden brown, about 5 minutes.

4 Remove from the heat, flip the chicken, and carefully drain and discard all but a few tablespoons of fat from the skillet. Add the garlic, rosemary, and tomatoes to the pan, place the foil-wrapped bricks on top of the chicken, and place in the oven. Cook until golden brown and the thickest part of the thigh reaches an internal temperature of 160°F, about 15 minutes. Carefully remove the bricks from the chicken.

5 *Meanwhile, make the salsa verde:* In a medium bowl, combine the parsley, shallot, capers, pepper flakes, anchovies, garlic, jalapeño, lemon zest, lemon juice, and olive oil. Season with a pinch of salt and a twist of pepper, toss to combine, and set aside for at least 15 minutes to marry the flavors.

6 Remove the chicken from the oven (discard the rosemary and garlic) and set aside to rest, loosely tented with foil, for 5 minutes.

7 Cut the chicken into two pieces by separating the breast from the leg, smash the roasted tomatoes over the top, and spoon on the salsa verde, and serve.

Reintroducing Sugar

Refined sugar beats me up more than any other ingredient. When I fall off the wagon, from eating ice cream, cheesecake, or pumpkin pie, I fall hard. But I still have a bit of a sweet tooth that needs to be satisfied every now and then, so I created recipes that take advantage of "softer" sugars like honey, maple syrup, coconut sugar, and date syrup. Using ripe in-season fruits also helps boost natural sweetness. The following recipes contain enough sweetness to please the palate, but lack any of the processed sugars that would trigger a response in people like me. If you're lucky, sugar won't cause you the sort of inflammation and pain that it does in me.

BROWN SUGAR OVERNIGHT OATS

SERVES 1

1¼ cups unsweetened almond milk

2 tablespoons light brown sugar

½ teaspoon ground cinnamon

1 cup old-fashioned rolled oats

2 tablespoons chia seeds

3 strawberries, hulled and quartered

In a medium bowl, whisk together the almond milk, brown sugar, and cinnamon. Add the oats and chia seeds and stir to combine. Transfer to a large mason jar or sealable container and refrigerate overnight. Serve topped with the strawberries.

FLOURLESS NUTELLA CREPES

SERVES 1

2 tablespoons sliced or slivered almonds

2 large eggs

1 small banana, sliced

Pinch of kosher salt

1 teaspoon coconut oil

2 tablespoons Nutella

1 Preheat the oven to 350°F.

2 Arrange the almonds on a sheet pan and cook until lightly toasted, about 8 minutes. Set aside.

3 In a blender, combine the eggs, banana, and salt and process until smooth.

4 Set a large nonstick skillet over medium-low heat. Add ½ teaspoon of the coconut oil and heat until melted. Make one crepe at a time by adding half of the batter to the skillet and immediately swirling the pan to form a thin, even layer. Cover and cook until the batter sets and the edges begin to brown, about 1 minute. Carefully remove the crepe from the pan, add 1 tablespoon of Nutella in a 1-inch-wide strip down the middle, and roll the crepe into a loose log. Cover to keep warm while you repeat the process with the remaining coconut oil, batter, and Nutella.

5 Serve topped with toasted almonds.

BBQ-GLAZED CARROTS
WITH ALMOND-CILANTRO QUINOA

SERVES 1

¼ cup sliced or slivered almonds

2 carrots, unpeeled and halved lengthwise

3 tablespoons extra-virgin olive oil

½ teaspoon grated fresh turmeric or ¼ teaspoon ground turmeric

Kosher salt and freshly ground black pepper

2 tablespoons Kansas City-Style BBQ Sauce (page 89) or your favorite sauce

1 tablespoon sherry vinegar

1 cup cooked Quinoa (page 245)

¼ cup finely chopped fresh cilantro

¼ cup finely chopped fresh flat-leaf parsley

2 scallions, thinly sliced

1 Preheat the oven to 350°F.

2 Arrange the almonds on a sheet pan and cook until lightly toasted, about 8 minutes. Set aside.

3 Prepare and preheat a gas or charcoal grill to create two heat zones: high and low. (Alternatively, preheat the oven to 300°F and line a sheet pan with foil.)

4 Coat the carrots on all sides with 1 tablespoon of the olive oil and season with the turmeric, a pinch of salt, and a twist of pepper. Place the carrots on the cool side of the grill (or on the lined sheet pan and into the oven) and cook until easily pierced by a fork, about 45 minutes. During the final 20 minutes, brush the carrots with BBQ sauce every 10 minutes.

5 Meanwhile, in a small bowl, whisk together the vinegar and remaining 2 tablespoons olive oil. Season with a pinch of salt and a twist of pepper. Add the quinoa, toasted almonds, cilantro, parsley, and scallions and toss to combine.

6 Transfer the salad to a plate, top with the carrots, and serve.

KANSAS CITY-STYLE BBQ SAUCE

MAKES 3 CUPS

This homemade barbecue sauce really is worth the effort, not only because it tastes a million times better than jarred, but also because we can control the type and quantity of sugars that go into it. Organic brown sugar, for example, has a nutritional leg up on refined white sugar typically found in grocery store brands.

3 tablespoons extra-virgin olive oil

1 small yellow onion, diced

3 garlic cloves, minced

Kosher salt

2 cups tomato sauce

¼ cup tomato paste

⅓ cup dark molasses

½ cup organic light brown sugar

⅓ cup raw apple cider vinegar

3 tablespoons yellow mustard

1 tablespoon chili powder

½ teaspoon cayenne pepper

Freshly ground black pepper

1 Set a nonreactive medium saucepan over medium heat. Add the olive oil and heat to shimmering, then add the onion, garlic, and a pinch of salt. Cook, stirring occasionally, until the vegetables soften, about 5 minutes.

2 Reduce the heat to medium-low, add the tomato sauce, tomato paste, molasses, brown sugar, vinegar, mustard, chili powder, and cayenne and whisk to combine. Season with a few pinches of salt and twists of black pepper. Simmer uncovered, stirring occasionally, for 30 minutes.

3 Remove from the heat, transfer to a blender or food processor, and process until smooth. Store for up to 2 weeks covered in the fridge or up to 1 month in the freezer.

NO DAIRY

Breakfasts

Lunches

Dinners

Snacks

Breakfasts

DATE, BANANA, WALNUT, AND OAT MILK SMOOTHIES

SERVES 2

I love my bacon-and-eggs breakfast more than anyone, but there are plenty of mornings when I don't have the time, hunger, or energy to prepare a full meal. But I still need the fuel to power through my day. Smoothies to the rescue! This one stars dates, which have an amazing caramel-like sweetness. The bananas and walnuts make this smoothie as creamy and fulfilling as an ice cream milkshake even though I use vegan, nondairy oat milk. You can use any nut milk—or even water—and still end up with a satisfying breakfast. Also, this recipe can be frozen into chill-pops for a fun, healthy summer treat.

1 cup walnuts

2 cups unsweetened oat milk

2 small bananas

6 dates, pitted and roughly chopped

¼ cup almond butter

1 teaspoon ground cinnamon

1 cup ice

1 Preheat the oven to 350°F.

2 Arrange the walnuts on a sheet pan and cook until lightly toasted, about 8 minutes. Transfer the walnuts to a cutting board and when cool enough to handle, roughly chop.

3 In a blender, combine the walnuts, oat milk, bananas, dates, almond butter, cinnamon, and ice and process until smooth. Drink immediately or store in the fridge for up to 2 days.

EGGS BAKED IN "CREAM"

SERVES 2

Baked eggs remove a lot of the anxiety and energy from preparing breakfast. This no-look, no-touch recipe lets the oven do all the work. Because these eggs keep their heat for so long after they come out of the oven, they are a great option for a stress-free family meal. When it comes to adding a lush creaminess to nondairy dishes, nothing comes close to oat milk. It's almost as good as real cream but with the added benefits of being vegan, nut-free, and soy-free.

¼ cup unsweetened oat milk

2 teaspoons fresh thyme leaves

¼ teaspoon freshly grated nutmeg

½ teaspoon hot sauce

4 large eggs

Kosher salt and freshly ground black pepper

2 slices whole-grain bread, toasted

1 Preheat the oven to 425°F.

2 In a small bowl, whisk together the oat milk, thyme, nutmeg, and hot sauce.

3 Arrange four 4-ounce ramekins on a sheet pan. Carefully crack an egg into each ramekin. Evenly divide the oat milk mixture among the ramekins and season each egg with a pinch of salt and a twist of pepper.

4 Cook until the whites are set but the yolks are still runny, about 10 minutes. If you prefer firmer yolks, cook for an additional 3 minutes.

5 Serve with whole-grain toast for dipping.

STRAWBERRY, COCONUT, AND ALMOND MILK SMOOTHIES

SERVES 2

I can't imagine a more heavenly flavor combo than strawberries, coconut, and honey. We balance out that sweetness with the tartness of fresh lime juice. The addition of toasted almonds brings body and creaminess while introducing powerful health benefits of monounsaturated fat (aka the good fat), antioxidants, and fiber. Coconut milk also is great in place of the almond milk. If you're concerned about vitamin D intake, you can look for fortified nut milks.

½ cup sliced or slivered almonds

2 cups unsweetened almond milk

2 cups frozen or hulled fresh strawberries

1 cup unsweetened shredded or flaked coconut

¼ cup raw honey

Juice of 2 limes

1 cup ice

1 Preheat the oven to 350°F.

2 Arrange the almonds on a sheet pan and cook until lightly toasted, about 8 minutes. Set aside.

3 In a blender, combine the almonds, almond milk, strawberries, coconut, honey, lime juice, and ice and process until smooth. Drink immediately or store in the fridge for up to 2 days.

SUNNY-SIDE UP EGGS
WITH RAPINI, HOT PEPPERS, AND SAUSAGE

SERVES 2

Is there any more versatile food than the egg? Even plain-old fried—aka sunny-side up—eggs can be prepared in different ways. Sometimes I prefer to cook them very gently, avoiding any color on the whites. Other times I crank the heat and really fry them to create crispy, golden-brown edges that add incredible flavor and texture. Slightly bitter rapini (broccoli rabe) goes great with sausage, but you can also use Swiss chard, arugula, or collard greens, all of which contain inflammation-fighting compounds present in cruciferous vegetables. If you have no issues with flour or gluten, enjoy this dish with a thick slice of grilled bread—especially if you like your egg yolks runny, as I do.

2 tablespoons extra-virgin olive oil

½ pound hot Italian sausage, removed from the casings if not bulk

2 cups chopped rapini (broccoli rabe)

2 Hungarian hot peppers, sliced

Kosher salt and freshly ground black pepper

6 large eggs

1 Set a large heavy-bottomed skillet over medium heat. Add 1 tablespoon of the olive oil and heat to shimmering, then add the sausage and cook until lightly browned, stirring occasionally to break up the meat, about 2 minutes. Add the rapini and peppers and season with a pinch of salt. Continue cooking until the vegetables soften, about 3 minutes. Transfer to a plate.

2 Return the skillet to medium heat. Add the remaining 1 tablespoon olive oil and heat to shimmering. Carefully crack the eggs into the pan and cook until the whites begin to brown around the edges, about 2 minutes. Season with a pinch of salt and a twist of pepper. Remove from the heat, add 1 tablespoon water, cover, and let steam for 30 seconds for runny yolks, 1 minute for medium-set yolks, and 1½ minutes for fully set yolks.

3 Place the sausage and peppers on a plate, top with eggs, and serve.

LEEK, ASPARAGUS, AND TARRAGON 5-MINUTE OMELET

SERVES 2

Omelets can be tricky to pull off—even for chefs! But this walk-away technique is a game-changer that produces light, fluffy, French-style omelets every single time. By letting the heat of the pan do much of the cooking off the stove, we eliminate the worry of overcooking the eggs or drying them out. Tarragon and eggs is such a classic pairing, but you can substitute any soft herb that you happen to have, like basil, cilantro, or parsley.

2 tablespoons extra-virgin olive oil

½ cup thinly sliced leeks, white and light-green parts only

1 cup thinly sliced asparagus

Kosher salt and freshly ground black pepper

6 large eggs

4 teaspoons finely chopped fresh tarragon

1 Set a large nonstick skillet over medium heat. Add 1 tablespoon of the olive oil followed by the leeks and asparagus. Season with a pinch of salt and cook, stirring occasionally, until the vegetables are aromatic and soft, about 2 minutes. Transfer half the vegetables to a plate and set aside until needed—leave the rest of the vegetables in the pan.

2 In a medium bowl, whisk together the eggs and a pinch of salt and a twist of pepper to thoroughly blend. Pour half the eggs into the skillet with the vegetables and cook, stirring constantly, until small, soft curds form, about 3 minutes. Shake the skillet to spread the eggs out into an even layer, cover, remove from the heat, and let sit for 5 minutes. Sprinkle on 2 teaspoons of the tarragon. Tilt the skillet and gently fold the omelet into thirds. Turn out onto a plate and keep warm while you repeat the process with the remaining 1 tablespoon olive oil, vegetable mixture, eggs, and tarragon.

CREAMY SCRAMBLED EGGS

SERVES 2

Scrambled eggs are often one of the first foods we learn to cook, even as a child. Everybody knows how to scramble an egg! But what if I told you that most people are doing it wrong? When you cook eggs very gently over low heat, you end up with a completely different dish. In place of dry and rubbery nuggets, this process produces creamy, custardy curds. Don't rush it; take your time and then enjoy the fruits of your patience afterward. The addition of full-fat coconut milk, which gets whisked into the eggs, makes these eggs as smooth as silk.

1 tablespoon extra-virgin olive oil

6 large eggs

½ cup unsweetened full-fat coconut milk

Kosher salt and freshly ground black pepper

2 tablespoons thinly sliced chives

2 tablespoons Faux Parmesan Cheese (page 248)

1 Set a large nonstick skillet over medium-low heat and add the olive oil.

2 In a medium bowl, whisk together the eggs and coconut milk. Season with a pinch of salt and a twist of pepper and pour into the skillet. Cook, stirring constantly, until small, soft curds form, about 3 minutes.

3 Stir in the chives and faux parmesan and serve.

Lunches

HUMMUS WITH VEGETABLES

MAKES 2 CUPS

Katie Pickens, our longtime culinary director and official cookbook recipe tester, is obsessed with hummus. She has been tinkering with this recipe weekly for months in an attempt to perfect it. What she found in her quest for light, fluffy, and supersmooth hummus was that adding extra tahini and some chilled chickpea liquid was an absolute game-changer. I think that you are going to love it as much as we do. At Middle Eastern restaurants, hummus is often garnished with za'atar, a nutty, herbal, and aromatic spice blend that is widely available in supermarkets and online. I recommend tracking some down and giving it a try.

1 (15-ounce) can chickpeas, 2 tablespoons liquid reserved and chilled, the rest discarded

8 garlic cloves, unpeeled

¼ cup fresh lemon juice

1½ teaspoons kosher salt

½ cup tahini

½ cup ice water

Extra-virgin olive oil, for serving

Paprika, za'atar, or sumac, for garnish

1 In a medium saucepan, combine the chickpeas and enough cold water to cover by a few inches. Bring to a boil over high heat, reduce the heat to medium to maintain a strong simmer, and cook until the chickpeas are completely soft and falling apart, about 1 hour.

2 Meanwhile, in a blender, combine the garlic (papery skins included), lemon juice, and salt and process to a pulpy puree. Transfer to a bowl and let sit for 5 minutes to allow the garlic to mellow. Strain through a fine-mesh sieve set over a medium bowl, discarding any solids. Add the tahini and whisk to combine. The mixture will be very thick. While continuously whisking, slowly add the ice water to produce a smooth sauce.

Assorted raw vegetables, for serving (such as cucumbers, radishes, bell peppers)

3 While still warm, drain the chickpeas (discarding the liquid) and add them to a blender along with the tahini mixture. Process until smooth, about 3 minutes. Add the chilled reserved chickpea liquid and process until very smooth and whipped, about 3 minutes. Transfer to a bowl and let sit at room temperature for 30 minutes to allow the hummus to thicken and mellow in flavor.

4 Garnish with olive oil and paprika, za'atar, or sumac. Serve with assorted raw vegetables. Store covered in the fridge for up to 5 days.

GROUND CHICKEN MEATBALLS
WITH PEANUT CILANTRO SAUCE

SERVES 2

Meatballs

1 pound ground chicken

4 scallions, thinly sliced

2 garlic cloves, minced

2 teaspoons grated fresh ginger

1 teaspoon ground coriander

2 tablespoons fish sauce

2 teaspoons tamari (wheat-free soy sauce)

2 tablespoons finely chopped fresh mint

4 tablespoons finely chopped fresh cilantro

Kosher salt and freshly ground black pepper

2 tablespoons extra-virgin olive oil

Peanut Cilantro Sauce

¼ cup unsalted roasted peanuts

1 garlic clove, sliced

1 cup fresh cilantro leaves and small stems

¼ cup extra-virgin olive oil

2 lime wedges, for serving

Even though my mom won't let me call these "meatballs" because they're made with chicken and not her classic trio of beef, pork, and veal, she does confess to liking them. These are not your average meatballs, I admit, but they are loaded with incredible umami-rich flavor thanks to the addition of tamari and fish sauce. The creamy peanut sauce puts them over the top, but I occasionally omit the sauce and serve the meatballs on top of a simple green salad for a lighter weeknight meal.

1 Preheat the oven to 425°F.

2 *Make the meatballs:* In a large bowl, combine the ground chicken, scallions, garlic, ginger, coriander, fish sauce, tamari, mint, and cilantro and stir to mix. Season with a pinch of salt and a twist of pepper. Divide the mixture into 8 equal portions and roll into meatballs about the size of a golf ball.

3 Set a large ovenproof skillet over medium heat. Add the olive oil and heat to shimmering, then add the meatballs. Cook until golden brown all over, about 3 minutes. Transfer the skillet to the oven and cook for 10 minutes.

4 *Make the peanut cilantro sauce:* In a blender or food processor, pulse the peanuts, garlic, and cilantro until the mixture has the consistency of coarse crumbs. With the machine running, slowly add the olive oil in a steady stream until just combined. Season with a pinch of salt and a twist of pepper.

5 Transfer the meatballs to a plate, top with peanut sauce, spritz with fresh lime juice, and serve.

POTATO PANCAKES
WITH BRUSSELS SPROUTS AND APPLE SALAD

SERVES 2

We grew up eating a ton of potato pancakes in my family, but applesauce was the typical topper of choice. This updated version swaps the sauce for a healthier Brussels sprouts and apple salad. For the crispiest results, rinse the shredded potatoes in cold water before draining and drying them really well in a kitchen towel.

2 medium russet potatoes, peeled and grated on the large holes of a box grater

2 scallions, thinly sliced

2 tablespoons finely chopped fresh dill

½ cup finely chopped fresh flat-leaf parsley, plus ½ cup whole leaves

1 large egg

2 tablespoons all-purpose flour

Kosher salt and freshly ground black pepper

4 tablespoons extra-virgin olive oil

2 tablespoons sherry vinegar

2 teaspoons Dijon mustard

½ teaspoon celery seeds

1 Granny Smith apple, peeled and cut into ⅛-inch-thick slices

1 cup shaved Brussels sprouts*

1 Wrap the grated potatoes in a kitchen towel and wring out (and discard) as much of the liquid as you can. Transfer the potatoes to a large bowl and add the scallions, dill, chopped parsley, egg, and flour. Season with a pinch of salt and a twist of pepper and toss to combine.

2 Set a large nonstick skillet over medium heat. Add 1 tablespoon of the olive oil and heat to shimmering, then add half of the potato mixture and smooth it out to an even layer with a spatula. Cook, without disturbing, until golden brown, about 3 minutes per side. Transfer to a plate and keep warm while you repeat the process with the remaining potato mixture and another 1 tablespoon olive oil.

3 Meanwhile, in a medium bowl, whisk together the vinegar, mustard, celery seeds, and remaining 2 tablespoons olive oil. Season with a pinch of salt and a twist of pepper. Add the apple, Brussels sprouts, and parsley leaves and toss to combine.

4 Place the potato pancakes on a plate, top with Brussels sprouts and apple salad, slice into wedges, and serve.

To shave the Brussels sprouts, use a food processor fitted with the slicing blade, a mandoline, or a very sharp knife and a steady hand.

SPAGHETTI POMODORO

SERVES 2

This is my go-to pomodoro, which comes together in about the time it takes to boil the spaghetti. I prefer to use canned San Marzano tomatoes because they are the next-best thing to garden-ripe fruit. Don't omit the herbs—both up front and at the end—because they add a ton of depth and brightness. If you want to chop up and add vegetables like zucchini, squash, or eggplant to the sauce, go right ahead. While tomatoes are an incredible source of antioxidants like vitamin C, you can never eat too many veggies!

Small bunch of fresh oregano

Small bunch of fresh thyme

5 tablespoons extra-virgin olive oil, plus more (optional) for serving

1 small yellow onion, finely chopped

4 garlic cloves, sliced

Kosher salt and freshly ground black pepper

½ teaspoon red pepper flakes

1 (28-ounce) can crushed San Marzano tomatoes

2 cups loosely packed fresh basil leaves

½ pound spaghetti

4 tablespoons Faux Parmesan Cheese (page 248), plus more (optional) for serving

1 Bundle up the oregano and thyme in butcher's twine and set aside.

2 Set a large saucepan over medium heat. Add 3 tablespoons of the olive oil, then add the onion, garlic, and a pinch of salt. Cook, stirring occasionally, until the vegetables soften, about 5 minutes. Add the pepper flakes and tomatoes. Season with a pinch of salt and a twist of pepper and add the herb bundle. Bring the sauce to a boil, then reduce the heat to medium-low to maintain a gentle simmer and cook for 15 minutes. Remove and discard the herb bundle, stir in the basil, and keep warm.

3 Meanwhile, add 3 tablespoons salt to a large pot of water and bring to a boil over high heat. Add the pasta and cook until just al dente, about 1 minute less than the package directions. Occasionally give the pasta a stir so it doesn't stick together. When the pasta is ready, scoop out and reserve ½ cup of the pasta water before draining the pasta in a colander.

4 Add the pasta to the pomodoro sauce along with the reserved pasta water. Add the faux parmesan and remaining 2 tablespoons olive oil and stir to combine. Top with more faux parmesan and olive oil at the table, if desired.

CRISPY RICE WITH ASPARAGUS, PEAS, AND MUSHROOMS

SERVES 2

Bobby Flay makes the greatest crispy rice dishes—always golden brown and crusty on the bottom, but perfectly moist and airy in the center. Whenever I see them on one of his restaurant menus, I am totally powerless to resist. This recipe is a little riff on some of that Flay magic. In spring, I go for tender green veggies like peas and asparagus, but in summer this would be just as great with zucchini, bell peppers, or hearty greens like kale. For the crispiest rice, make sure the cooked rice is chilled before using, so have some ready and waiting in the fridge.

4 tablespoons extra-virgin olive oil

1 cup sliced cremini mushrooms

1 cup cooked rice (I use brown rice, see page 246)

½ cup fresh or frozen peas

½ cup thinly sliced asparagus

1 teaspoon ground coriander

Kosher salt and freshly ground black pepper

2 tablespoons finely chopped fresh flat-leaf parsley

2 large eggs

1 Set a large nonstick skillet over medium heat. Add 3 tablespoons of the olive oil and heat to shimmering, then add the mushrooms and rice. Cook, stirring occasionally, until the mushrooms and rice turn crisp and light golden brown, about 3 minutes. Add the peas, asparagus, and coriander and season with a pinch of salt and a twist of pepper. Continue cooking until the vegetables soften, about 2 minutes. Remove from the heat, stir in the parsley, and divide the rice between two plates.

2 Return the skillet to medium heat. Add the remaining 1 tablespoon olive oil and heat to shimmering. Carefully crack the eggs into the pan and cook until the whites begin to brown around the edges, about 2 minutes. Season with a pinch of salt and a twist of pepper. Remove from the heat, add 1 tablespoon water, cover, and let steam for 30 seconds for runny yolks, 1 minute for medium-set yolks, and 1½ minutes for fully set yolks.

3 Place the eggs on the crispy rice and serve.

BREAD SALAD WITH TOMATO, BASIL, AND RED ONION

SERVES 2

This is a pretty classic take on panzanella, the Italian salad starring bread and tomatoes. I make these salads all the time as a way to use up any day- (or two) old bread. But in this case, I start with bakery-fresh bread and toast it to golden-brown goodness with olive oil. This is not a time for grocery-store sandwich bread—artisan-style breads like sourdough, ciabatta, or even baguettes are much better at standing up to the dressing. In late summer, when I am swimming in juicy-ripe tomatoes, this salad really shines, but this recipe works just as well at other times of the year by using always-in-season cherry tomatoes.

8 tablespoons extra-virgin olive oil

2 garlic cloves, grated

Kosher salt and freshly ground black pepper

2 cups ¼-inch rustic bread cubes

2 tablespoons red wine vinegar

2 teaspoons Dijon mustard

¼ teaspoon dried oregano

2 large tomatoes, diced

½ small red onion, thinly sliced

2 cups loosely packed fresh basil leaves

Crunchy sea salt, for serving

1 Preheat the oven to 350°F.

2 In a large bowl, combine 4 tablespoons of the olive oil and the garlic. Season with a pinch of salt and a twist of pepper. Add the bread cubes and toss to evenly coat. Arrange the bread in an even layer on a sheet pan and cook until toasted and golden brown, about 15 minutes. Allow to cool slightly before adding them to the vinaigrette in the next step.

3 In the same bowl, whisk together the vinegar, mustard, oregano, and remaining 4 tablespoons olive oil. Season with a pinch of salt and a twist of pepper. Add the tomatoes and onion and toss to combine. Add the bread cubes and basil and gently fold to combine.

4 Transfer the salad to a plate, garnish with crunchy sea salt and pepper, and serve.

Dinners

CREAMY BAKED PUMPKIN MAC AND CHEESE

SERVES 2

Did somebody request a creamy, decadent, dairy-free mac and cheese? This dish looks, tastes, and eats so much like "real" macaroni and cheese that even picky eaters will be fooled. The secret is pumpkin puree, which adds a silky richness. The pumpkin's subtle sweetness also balances out the natural saltiness of the faux parmesan. We make this for Thanksgiving when we usually have plenty of pumpkin puree on hand. Supposedly, it is reserved for the few family members who can't tolerate dairy, but believe me, everyone tries to steal a bite! If you really want to fool the kiddos, swap the rigatoni for the more traditional elbow macaroni.

4 tablespoons panko bread crumbs

2 tablespoons thinly sliced chives

10 tablespoons Faux Parmesan Cheese (page 248)

Kosher salt and freshly ground black pepper

½ pound rigatoni pasta

3 cups unsweetened oat milk

1 teaspoon freshly grated nutmeg

1 Preheat the oven to 350°F.

2 Arrange the panko on a sheet pan and cook until lightly toasted, about 5 minutes. Transfer the panko to a medium bowl. Add the chives and 2 tablespoons of the faux parmesan and toss to combine. Set aside until needed.

3 Add 3 tablespoons salt to a large pot of water and bring to a boil over high heat. Add the pasta and cook until just al dente, about 1 minute less than the package directions. Occasionally give the pasta a stir so it doesn't stick together.

1 teaspoon chipotle powder

1 teaspoon smoked paprika

½ cup canned pure pumpkin puree

2 teaspoons Dijon mustard

2 large egg yolks

2 teaspoons hot sauce

4 Meanwhile, in a medium saucepan whisk together the oat milk, nutmeg, chipotle powder, and paprika. Season with a pinch of salt and a twist of pepper. Bring to a simmer over medium heat and cook until the liquid has reduced by half, about 15 minutes. Add the pumpkin, mustard, egg yolks, and hot sauce and whisk to combine. Remove from the heat and stir in the drained pasta and remaining 8 tablespoons faux parmesan.

5 Serve topped with the toasted panko mixture.

GRILLED RIB EYE
WITH CRISPY MUSHROOMS

SERVES 2

I can't even type these words without drooling! When it comes to last meals, this would be near the top of my list. To me, rib-eye steaks have the perfect amount of intermuscular marbling to produce the perfect level of tenderness without sacrificing any of the great beefy flavor. I know great rib-eye steak is not cheap, but I always recommend spending a little more for the good stuff and enjoying it less frequently as a treat. The mushroom and spinach salad lends the dish a real chophouse feel, while providing more health benefits than a jog around the park. Bust out a great bottle of red wine (assuming alcohol isn't a trigger) and celebrate the simple things! That said, this recipe would be almost as delicious with flank or skirt steak.

2 rib-eye steaks
(14 ounces each),
preferably dry-aged

Kosher salt and freshly
ground black pepper

2 tablespoons Dijon
mustard

4 tablespoons extra-
virgin olive oil

4 cups sliced cremini
mushrooms

1 cup fresh or frozen corn
kernels

4 scallions, thinly sliced

2 tablespoons sherry
vinegar

2 cups packed thinly
sliced spinach leaves

1 Preheat a grill or grill pan to medium-high heat.

2 Season the steaks on both sides with salt and pepper. Evenly coat the steaks with the mustard and drizzle with 1 tablespoon of the olive oil. Cook until nicely charred and medium-rare, about 3 minutes per side. Set aside to rest, loosely tented with foil, for 5 minutes before slicing.

3 Meanwhile, set a large skillet over medium heat. Add the remaining 3 tablespoons olive oil and heat to shimmering, then add the mushrooms. Shake the skillet to spread them out into an even layer. Cook, without stirring, until the bottoms gets crispy, about 5 minutes. Add the corn and scallions and season with a pinch of salt and a twist of pepper. Continue cooking until the corn begins to soften, about 2 minutes. Remove from the heat and stir in the vinegar and spinach.

4 Divide the spinach/mushroom salad between two plates. Place the sliced rib eye on top of the salad and serve.

GRILLED CHICKEN THIGHS
WITH PEAR CHUTNEY

SERVES 2

Once you taste this chutney, you are going to want to spoon it over everything. This savory condiment is sweet and sour and loaded with earthy spice. There is almost no dish that a sprinkle or three of Old Bay will not improve, this chutney included. The famous spice blend shines thanks to a balance of mustard, bay leaf, celery salt, paprika, and a dozen other ingredients. When I get my hands on some beautiful ripe pears in the fall, I will make double batches of this chutney and store it in the fridge, where it will stay good for weeks. Spoon it over grilled meats, spread it on a sandwich, or use it as a hot dog topping. There is no wrong answer! If you can't unearth currants, try this recipe with golden raisins, dates, or dried cherries.

4½ tablespoons extra-virgin olive oil

2 teaspoons Old Bay seasoning

2 teaspoons smoked paprika

Grated zest of 2 limes

4 bone-in, skin-on chicken thighs

Kosher salt and freshly ground black pepper

2 tablespoons sherry vinegar

Juice of 1 lime

¼ cup packed light brown sugar

1 tablespoon grated fresh ginger

1 In a small bowl, whisk together 4 tablespoons of the olive oil, the Old Bay, smoked paprika, and lime zest.

2 Season both sides of the chicken with a few pinches of salt and twists of pepper and place in a gallon-size zip-top bag. Add the marinade and refrigerate for at least 2 hours, but up to overnight.

3 Set a medium saucepan over medium heat. Add the vinegar, lime juice, brown sugar, and ¼ cup water. Bring to a simmer, whisking to dissolve the sugar. Add the ginger, jalapeño, coriander, and currants. Continue cooking until the liquid has reduced by half and reaches a syrup-like consistency, about 5 minutes.

4 Reduce the heat to low, add the pears, season with a pinch of salt, and continue cooking until the pears are very soft, about 15 minutes.

5 Preheat a grill or grill pan to medium-high heat.

1 jalapeño, seeded and finely chopped

½ teaspoon ground coriander

2 tablespoons dried currants

1 Bartlett pear, peeled, cored, and diced

1 cup arugula

Juice of ½ lemon

6 Remove the chicken from the bag, allowing most of the marinade to drip off (discard the marinade). Set the chicken skin-side down on the grill and cook, uncovered, without moving, until nicely charred, about 8 minutes. Flip and continue cooking until the chicken reaches an internal temperature of 160°F, about 6 minutes. Remove the chicken from the grill and set aside to rest, loosely tented with foil, for 5 minutes.

7 Meanwhile, in a medium bowl, combine the arugula, lemon juice, and remaining ½ tablespoon olive oil. Season with a pinch of salt and a twist of pepper. Toss to combine.

8 Transfer the chicken to a plate, spoon on some pear chutney, top with arugula salad, and serve.

THAI SHRIMP CURRY

SERVES 2

This is a very quick, simple, and impressive curry that comes together in no time thanks to the jarred red curry paste (I use Thai Kitchen brand). I prefer my curries hot and spicy, so I often toss in a few more jalapeños—seeds and all—or a pinch of red pepper flakes. If you want to substitute the shrimp for a different seafood, scallops or cubed fish like salmon, tuna, or cod would be amazing. Serve this dish with plenty of steamed white or brown rice to soak up the delicious sauce.

4 tablespoons extra-virgin olive oil

1 pound large shrimp, peeled and deveined

Kosher salt and freshly ground black pepper

2 cups sliced snow peas or sugar snap peas

4 scallions, thinly sliced

2 garlic cloves, sliced

2 tablespoons grated fresh ginger

2 jalapeños, seeded and finely chopped

2 cups unsweetened full-fat coconut milk

Grated zest and juice of 2 limes

4 tablespoons Thai red curry paste

2 tablespoons light brown sugar

½ cup chopped toasted unsalted peanuts

Cooked rice, for serving

1 Set a large skillet over medium heat. Add 2 tablespoons of the olive oil and heat to shimmering, then add the shrimp in a single layer. Season with a pinch of salt and a twist of pepper and cook until the shrimp turn pink on one side, about 2 minutes. Flip and continue cooking until just pink throughout, about 1 minute. Transfer the shrimp to a plate and set aside.

2 Add the remaining 2 tablespoons olive oil to the pan, followed by the snow peas, scallions, garlic, ginger, and jalapeños. Season with a pinch of salt and a twist of pepper. Cook, stirring occasionally, until the vegetables are aromatic and soft, about 3 minutes.

3 Meanwhile, in a medium bowl, whisk together the coconut milk, lime zest, lime juice, curry paste, and brown sugar.

4 Add the coconut milk mixture to the skillet, bring to a simmer, and cook until reduced by half, about 5 minutes. Remove from the heat, stir in the shrimp and peanuts, and serve over rice.

POMEGRANATE-GLAZED SALMON

SERVES 2

Pomegranate molasses is not as sweet as you might think—it adds such a compelling and unique tart and earthy flavor to dishes that I keep trying to find new ways to use it (especially since it stays good forever in the pantry!). I discovered that it is the perfect partner to salmon because its sharpness cuts right through the fish's richness. Pomegranate also happens to be one of the most powerful antioxidants around. For those who might be intimidated by cooking fish, this oven-roast method is essentially goof proof. Just dust off your trusty thermometer to know when it's done. This appealing glaze can also be used with chicken, turkey, or pork, but you'll need to adjust the cooking time and final temperature.

2 tablespoons pomegranate molasses

1 tablespoon tamari (wheat-free soy sauce)

1 tablespoon Dijon mustard

2 skinless salmon fillets (8 ounces each)

2 tablespoons extra-virgin olive oil

2 tablespoons chopped raw cashews

1 cup basmati rice

Kosher salt and freshly ground black pepper

2 scallions, thinly sliced

2 tablespoons finely chopped fresh cilantro

1 Preheat the oven to 325°F.

2 In a medium bowl, whisk together the pomegranate molasses, tamari, and mustard.

3 Place the salmon in a 9 × 13-inch baking dish, evenly coat both sides with the marinade, and cook until the thickest part reaches an internal temperature of 120°F for medium-rare or 130°F if you prefer more well-done and really flaky fish, about 30 minutes.

4 Meanwhile, set a medium saucepan over medium-low heat. Add the olive oil followed by the cashews and cook until aromatic and golden brown, about 30 seconds. Stir in the rice. Add 2 cups water and bring to a boil. Season with a pinch of salt and a twist of pepper. Cover, reduce the heat to low to maintain a gentle simmer, and cook for 10 minutes. Remove from the heat and let stand, covered, for 5 minutes.

5 Fluff the rice with a fork, stir in the scallions and cilantro, and divide it between two plates. Top with the salmon and serve.

PENNE WITH OLIVE OIL AND BROCCOLI

SERVES 2

Simple is often best, as evidenced by this pasta, which has no spare parts. All it takes is a little of the starchy pasta water to create a rich, flavorful sauce when blended with the garlic and faux parmesan—you'd swear there was dairy here! This recipe is endlessly adaptable, so try it with different pastas and different vegetables, such as broccoli rabe, asparagus, or cauliflower. Personally, I love the healthiness and slight crunch from crisp-tender broccoli. When it comes to pasta, sometimes the less complicated the recipe is, the better.

Kosher salt and freshly ground black pepper

½ pound penne pasta

6 tablespoons extra-virgin olive oil

2 cups broccoli florets and tender stems

6 garlic cloves, sliced

½ teaspoon red pepper flakes

½ cup Faux Parmesan Cheese (page 248)

1 Add 3 tablespoons salt to a large pot of water and bring to a boil over high heat. Add the pasta and cook until just al dente, about 1 minute less than the package directions. Occasionally give the pasta a stir so it doesn't stick together. Scoop out and reserve 1 cup of the pasta water before draining the pasta.

2 Set a large skillet over medium heat. Add 4 tablespoons of the olive oil and heat to shimmering, then add the broccoli. Season with a pinch of salt and a twist of pepper. Cook until the broccoli begins to soften and brown, about 3 minutes. Add the garlic and pepper flakes and continue cooking until the garlic is aromatic, about 2 minutes. Add the reserved pasta water and bring to a simmer. Stir in the cooked pasta. Season with a pinch of salt and a twist of pepper.

3 Remove from the heat, stir in the faux parmesan and remaining 2 tablespoons olive oil, and serve.

Snacks

With dukkah and me, it was love at first taste. This complex Middle Eastern blend of nuts, seeds, and spices is a great addition to soups, salads, and grilled fish. But I use it to add flavor and texture to creamy and refreshing coconut yogurt. You're also going to go love the Banana Nice-Cream (page 128), which is ridiculously easy and yet every bit as dreamy-delicious as real ice cream. Try blending in some peanut butter, stirring in a handful of ripe berries, or topping with crunchy nuts. Lastly, we came up with a no-bake version of granola bars that will last for up to 2 weeks, so you can stash a few in the car, at the office, or in a backpack.

NO-BAKE GRANOLA BITES

MAKES 10 BITES

1 tablespoon extra-virgin olive oil

1 cup old-fashioned rolled oats

½ cup roughly chopped pecans

½ cup unsweetened shredded coconut

3 tablespoons chia seeds

¼ cup unsalted roasted sunflower seeds

Pinch of kosher salt

½ cup chopped dried cherries or cranberries

3 tablespoons coconut oil

2 tablespoons raw honey

2 tablespoons almond butter

1 Grease 12 cups of a muffin tin with the olive oil.

2 In a large bowl, combine the oats, pecans, coconut, chia seeds, sunflower seeds, salt, and dried fruit and toss to combine.

3 Set a small saucepan over low heat. Add the coconut oil, honey, and almond butter. When melted, transfer to the bowl of dry ingredients and stir to thoroughly combine.

4 Place ⅓ cup oat mixture into each muffin tin. With the bottom of the measuring cup, flatten the granola in each cup to form a compact puck. Cover and refrigerate until cold and firm, about 2 hours.

5 Run a knife around the perimeter of each muffin tin to pop out the granola bites. Store in an airtight container for up to 2 weeks in the fridge or freezer.

BANANA NICE-CREAM

SERVES 1

1 ripe banana, sliced and frozen firm

2 tablespoons nondairy milk (I use unsweetened almond milk)

1 tablespoon chopped almonds

In a blender or food processor, combine the frozen banana and milk and blend until completely smooth and whipped. Garnish with almonds and serve immediately.

COCONUT YOGURT
WITH DUKKAH AND GRAPES

SERVES 1

¼ **cup salted roasted pistachios**

1 teaspoon coriander seeds

½ **teaspoon black peppercorns**

1 tablespoon sesame seeds

1 cup unsweetened coconut yogurt

⅓ **cup halved red or green grapes**

1 In a blender or food processor, pulse the pistachios, coriander seeds, and black peppercorns until the mixture has the consistency of fine crumbs. Transfer to a medium bowl, add the sesame seeds, and stir the dukkah to combine.

2 Top the yogurt with grapes, sprinkle on 1 tablespoon dukkah, and serve. Store the remaining dukkah in an airtight container for up to 1 month in the cupboard.

NO FLOUR

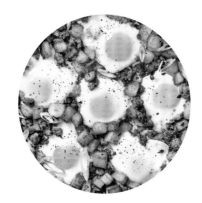

Breakfasts

Lunches

Dinners

Snacks

Breakfasts

SAUSAGE, EGG, AND POTATO SKILLET

SERVES 2

As a kid, I always loved a breakfast skillet—either when it was my dad cooking it for the family on Saturdays or when we all went out to eat after church on Sundays. All these years later and my appreciation for them has not faded. The only rule for these convenient all-in-one-pan dishes is to combine compatible ingredients, and nothing goes together better than sausage, eggs, and potatoes! But breakfast skillets are super flexible, so feel free to swap out the sausage for bacon, ham, or even vegetables if you feel like going meat-free.

2 tablespoons extra-virgin olive oil

½ pound sweet Italian sausage, removed from the casings if not bulk

2 cups diced russet potato

Kosher salt and freshly ground black pepper

4 scallions, thinly sliced

2 teaspoons fresh thyme leaves, roughly chopped

6 large eggs

1 Preheat the oven to 350°F.

2 Set a large heavy-bottomed skillet over medium-high heat. Add the olive oil and heat to shimmering, then add the sausage. Cook, stirring with a wooden spoon to break up the meat, until lightly browned, about 3 minutes. Add the potato, season with a pinch of salt and a twist of pepper, and continue cooking until the potatoes are tender and golden brown, about 5 minutes. Add the scallions and thyme and stir to combine. Make 6 shallow depressions in the sausage and potato mixture and carefully crack an egg into each one.

3 Transfer the skillet to the oven and cook until the egg whites are set but the yolks are still runny, about 10 minutes.

4 Serve from the skillet.

LIZZIE'S GRANOLA

MAKES 5 CUPS

I know I tend to hog all the attention, but the truth is Lizzie makes certain dishes much better than I do. One of her specialties is granola. Her classic formula has the perfect proportion of whole grains, nuts, and spices, and it's not cloyingly sweet like many of the commercial ones available. This protein-packed granola will last for a month in an airtight container, so consider doubling or tripling the recipe—even if you're not planning to climb a mountain or hike the Appalachian Trail.

2 cups old-fashioned rolled oats

1 cup unsweetened flaked or shredded coconut

½ cup slivered almonds

½ cup raw cashews

2 tablespoons chia seeds

4 tablespoons extra-virgin olive oil

4 tablespoons raw honey

1 teaspoon ground cinnamon

1 teaspoon kosher salt

1 cup dried fruit (figs, dates, apricots, cranberries, cherries)

1 Preheat the oven to 325°F.

2 In a medium bowl, combine the oats, coconut, almonds, cashews, chia seeds, oil, honey, cinnamon, and salt and toss to coat. Spread evenly on a baking sheet and cook, stirring once halfway through, until lightly golden brown, about 20 minutes.

3 Let cool completely on the baking sheet.

4 Stir in the dried fruit and serve. If not using right away, don't add the fruit until serving. The granola will keep for up to 1 month in an airtight container at room temperature.

POACHED EGGS
WITH CHARRED ONION AND MORNAY SAUCE

SERVES 2

Don't be intimidated by the poached eggs and fancy-sounding sauce in this recipe; this dish is not as complicated as it looks. I know some people get a little anxious about poaching eggs, but I say give it a whirl (literally, because that's the key to perfect poaching, as described below). If you prefer to substitute scrambled, fried, or over-easy eggs for the poached eggs, go for it. Also, Mornay sauce is just a posh way of saying "cheese sauce," so don't let that frighten you. It's a great technique to learn because it's the secret to amazing macaroni and cheese, but it's also great drizzled over roasted broccoli or served alongside poached salmon and grilled meats. I think Gruyère is the perfect cheese for this, but Swiss, parmesan, or even cheddar would work.

1 tablespoon unsalted butter

1 tablespoon all-purpose flour

½ teaspoon freshly grated nutmeg

1 cup whole milk

1 cup shredded Gruyère cheese

1 teaspoon Dijon mustard

Kosher salt and freshly ground black pepper

1 tablespoon extra-virgin olive oil

2 small onions, cut into 1-inch-thick rings

2 tablespoons distilled white vinegar

4 large eggs

1 Preheat the oven to 350°F.

2 Set a medium saucepan over medium heat. Add the butter and allow it to melt, then add the flour and whisk to blend. Add the nutmeg and, while constantly whisking, slowly add the milk. Cook, whisking occasionally, until smooth and thickened, about 5 minutes. Add the Gruyère and mustard and whisk until the cheese has melted. Taste and adjust for seasoning, adding salt and pepper as needed. Cover and set aside.

3 Set a large ovenproof skillet over medium-high heat. Add the olive oil and heat to shimmering, then add the onion rings. Cook, without moving, until nicely browned, about 3 minutes. Flip and continue cooking until the other side is browned, about 2 minutes. Season with a pinch of salt and a twist of pepper. Transfer the pan to the oven and cook until the onion is tender, about 8 minutes.

4 Meanwhile, in a medium saucepan, combine 4 cups water and the vinegar and bring to a strong simmer over medium-high heat. Crack each egg into its own little bowl. With a spoon, create a large (but gentle) whirlpool in the simmering water by stirring in one direction around the perimeter of the pan. Gently lower the eggs into the center of the pan. Poach, untouched, until the eggs are set enough to be lifted out of the water without breaking but the yolks are still runny, about 3 minutes. Gently lift the eggs out of the water with a slotted spoon and transfer to a paper towel to remove excess water.

5 Transfer the onions to a plate, top each with a poached egg, spoon on the Mornay sauce, and serve.

SWEET POTATO FRITTATA

SERVES 2

It's funny, but I never even knew about sweet potatoes as a kid. Growing up, there was only one kind of potato: white! Over the years I've grown to appreciate the full family of potatoes, including sweet potatoes, those familiar orange-fleshed tubers that boast a subtle natural sweetness. While we typically think of sweet potatoes (a root veggie, really) as autumn crops, I keep a stash of them in my pantry all year long. They can be used in place of ordinary spuds in most recipes, and they have incredible health benefits, not the least of which is a heaping supply of beta-carotene, the antioxidant beneficial to eye health.

6 large eggs, beaten

1 teaspoon grated fresh turmeric or ⅓ teaspoon ground turmeric

1 teaspoon chipotle powder

Kosher salt and freshly ground black pepper

2 tablespoons extra-virgin olive oil

2 small sweet potatoes, peeled and grated

1 cup thinly sliced bell pepper

4 scallions, thinly sliced

1 Preheat the oven to 350°F.

2 In a medium bowl, combine the eggs, turmeric, and chipotle. Season with a pinch of salt and a twist of pepper and stir to combine.

3 Set a large ovenproof nonstick skillet over medium heat. Add the olive oil and heat to shimmering, then add the sweet potatoes, bell pepper, and a pinch of salt and cook until the vegetables begin to soften, about 5 minutes. Add the scallions and stir. Pour in the egg mixture, transfer the skillet to the oven, and cook until the eggs are set and lightly golden brown, about 5 minutes.

4 Transfer to a serving plate and serve.

BREAKFAST RICE PUDDING

SERVES 2

I can't recall a time when we visited my yiayia's house that she didn't have rice pudding waiting for us. Ever since I was a child, rice pudding has been a comfort food that conjures up cherished memories of time spent with my grandmother. While our family always enjoyed rice pudding as a special dessert, the creamy porridge is equally appropriate for breakfast. Top it with whatever fresh fruit you have on hand. And don't forget the nuts for crunch! This indulgent pudding can be enjoyed warm, cold, or at room temp. I use Arborio rice because it's starchy and that's what my yiayia used, but feel free to use another white rice.

¼ cup sliced or slivered almonds

2 (15-ounce) cans unsweetened full-fat coconut milk

½ cup Arborio rice

6 tablespoons raw honey

1 teaspoon ground cinnamon

Kosher salt

1 teaspoon vanilla extract

½ cup hulled and quartered strawberries

1 Preheat the oven to 350°F.

2 Arrange the almonds on a sheet pan and cook until lightly toasted, about 8 minutes. Set aside.

3 Set a medium saucepan over medium-low heat and add the coconut milk, ½ cup water, the rice, honey, cinnamon, and a pinch of salt. Bring to a simmer, stir, cover, and cook until the rice is tender and creamy, about 20 minutes.

4 Remove from the heat and let stand, covered, for 5 minutes. Add the vanilla, top with strawberries and almonds, and serve warm or at room temperature.

YOGURT DATE SMOOTHIES

SERVES 2

The busier I tend to get, the more breakfast smoothies I seem to make. These easy meals-in-a-glass are filling and substantial enough to tide me over on those days when work—or life—prevents me from enjoying a proper lunch. The tartness of the Greek yogurt is tamed by the sweet dates and rich, creamy banana. If you want to make this recipe dairy-free, swap out the Greek yogurt for a coconut milk-based one like Cocojune.

2 cups plain whole-milk Greek yogurt

2 small bananas

½ cup chopped pitted dates (I prefer Medjool)

2 tablespoons raw honey

1 cup ice

In a blender, combine all of the ingredients and process until smooth. Drink immediately or store in the fridge for up to 2 days.

Lunches

BLACK BEAN SOUP

SERVES 2

1 tablespoon toasted
sesame oil

½ cup diced yellow onion

½ cup diced red bell
pepper

Kosher salt and freshly
ground black pepper

2 garlic cloves, sliced

2 tablespoons finely
chopped fresh ginger

1 tablespoon white miso

1¾ cups unsweetened
full-fat coconut milk or
other nondairy milk

1 (15-ounce) can black
beans, drained and
rinsed

Juice of 1 lime

2 tablespoons finely
chopped fresh cilantro

Believe it or not, I did not raise a single spoon of black bean soup to my mouth until after I graduated from culinary school. We just didn't have it growing up, for some reason. It wasn't until my aunt Mary took me to eat at the Mansion on Turtle Creek, the famous Dallas restaurant, which was run at the time by chef Dean Fearing, that I had my first taste. That bowl of black bean soup will always be burned into my taste memories as the best of the best. Nobody can make it better than Dean, but this vegan version made with miso, toasted sesame oil, and coconut milk comes close.

1 Set a medium saucepan over medium-high heat. Add the sesame oil followed by the onion, bell pepper, a pinch of salt, and a twist of pepper. Cook until the vegetables begin to soften, about 3 minutes. Add the garlic and ginger and cook until aromatic, about 2 minutes. Add the miso, milk, and black beans. Bring to a strong simmer and cook, partially covered, until the vegetables are very tender, about 20 minutes.

2 Carefully transfer the soup to a blender or food processor and puree until smooth. If the soup looks thicker than you'd like, add a little water until you reach the desired consistency.

3 Transfer the soup to bowls, stir in the lime juice, and serve topped with the cilantro.

TRADITIONAL COBB SALAD

SERVES 2 WITH LEFTOVER DRESSING

It was always a great day when my mom would take me out to lunch as a kid. And if the restaurant we visited had a Cobb salad on the menu, even better. To this day, I remember how mature I felt just by ordering that "fancy" salad, with its distinctive stripes of toppings of hard-boiled eggs, crispy bacon, avocado, and crumbled blue cheese. The key for me these days is this homemade dressing, made with just enough Dijon mustard to tie it all together. The leftover dressing (a generous ½ cup) will keep in the fridge for up to 2 weeks and can be used on any kind of salad.

Dressing (makes ¾ cup)

1 large egg yolk

1 tablespoon Dijon mustard

1 tablespoon Worcestershire sauce

Juice of ½ lemon

1 tablespoon red wine vinegar

1 garlic clove, minced

Kosher salt and freshly ground black pepper

¼ cup extra-virgin olive oil

Salad

1 (6-ounce) bone-in, skin-on chicken breast

1 tablespoon extra-virgin olive oil

Kosher salt and freshly ground black pepper

6 slices bacon

1 *Make the dressing:* In a small bowl, whisk together the egg yolk, mustard, Worcestershire sauce, lemon juice, vinegar, and garlic. Season with a pinch of salt and a twist of pepper. While continuously whisking, slowly add the olive oil in a steady stream. Set aside.

2 Preheat the oven to 450°F. Line two sheet pans with foil.

3 *Make the salad:* Coat both sides of the chicken with the olive oil, season with a pinch of salt and a twist of pepper, and arrange skin-side up on one of the sheet pans. Cook until the chicken reaches an internal temperature of 160°F, about 35 minutes. Remove the chicken from the oven and set aside to rest, loosely tented with foil, for 10 minutes. When cool enough to handle, cut the chicken into bite-size pieces, discarding the skin and bones.

4 Reduce the oven temperature to 425°F.

5 Place the bacon on the other sheet pan and cook until crisp, about 10 minutes. Transfer to a plate lined with paper towels to drain. When cool enough to handle, roughly chop.

6 Place the eggs in a small saucepan, cover with cold water by 1 inch, and bring to a boil over high heat. Remove from the heat, cover the pan, and set aside for 11 minutes. Drain

2 large eggs

4 cups ½-inch-thick sliced romaine heart leaves

½ cup halved cherry tomatoes

½ avocado, sliced

4 tablespoons crumbled blue cheese

and chill the egg in cold water for 1 minute. When the eggs are cool, peel and cut into wedges.

7 In a large bowl, toss the romaine with 3 tablespoons of the salad dressing, a pinch of salt, and a twist of pepper. Transfer the lettuce to a plate and in a classic ribbon pattern, top with bacon, eggs, tomato, avocado, blue cheese, and chicken, and serve.

CRUNCHY CHICKEN SALAD

SERVES 2

This is one of those dishes that I can eat every single day and never grow bored. The colorful salad, made with red peppers, red cabbage, and scallions, is light, flavorful, and filling enough for lunch or dinner. If you haven't yet made the switch from regular soy sauce to tamari, I suggest you give it a try. Not only is tamari typically wheat-free (and thus gluten-free), it has a deeper, richer taste while being less aggressively salty. For a slightly more elegant preparation, shred the cooked chicken into strands using two forks (there's nothing wrong with using a knife to chop it into small chunks, either). I always prefer to start with roasted bone-in, skin-on chicken because the meat tastes better, but boneless, skinless breasts (or thighs) are fine, too—as is a rotisserie chicken if you don't have time to roast your own.

½ cup sliced or slivered almonds

2 bone-in, skin-on chicken breasts (6 ounces each)

3 tablespoons extra-virgin olive oil

Kosher salt and freshly ground black pepper

1 cup sliced peppers (I use red bell peppers)

4 scallions, thinly sliced

1 cup thinly sliced red cabbage

1 cup thinly sliced carrot

2 tablespoons sesame seeds

2 tablespoons tamari (wheat-free soy sauce)

Juice of 1 lime

1 Preheat the oven to 350°F.

2 Arrange the almonds on a sheet pan and cook until lightly toasted, about 8 minutes. Set aside.

3 Increase the oven temperature to 450°F. Line a sheet pan with foil.

4 Coat both sides of the chicken with 1 tablespoon of the olive oil and season with a pinch of salt and a twist of black pepper. Arrange skin-side up on the sheet pan. Cook until the chicken reaches an internal temperature of 160°F, about 35 minutes. Remove the chicken from the oven and set aside to rest, loosely tented with foil, for 10 minutes. When cool enough to handle, shred the chicken into bite-size pieces, discarding the skin and bones.

5 Meanwhile, in a medium bowl, combine the bell peppers, scallions, cabbage, carrot, almonds, sesame seeds, tamari, remaining 2 tablespoons olive oil, and the lime juice. Season with a pinch of salt and a twist of pepper and toss to combine. Add the chicken, toss, and serve.

CLAMS WITH ESCAROLE, GARLIC, AND TOMATO

SERVES 2

This is easily one of my top-five recipes in this book. There's just something special about the combination of briny clams, slightly bitter escarole, and the subtle kick of hot pepper flakes. Live clams are easier than ever to find at grocery stores, and cooking them is not at all complicated—it takes just a few minutes. When clams open during cooking, they release delicious juices that combine with the tomatoes to produce an amazing sauce. I like the slight bitterness that escarole (a leafy almost lettuce-like green) brings to this dish, but feel free to substitute a hearty green like kale, Swiss chard, or mustard greens.

24 littleneck clams, scrubbed

2 cups halved cherry tomatoes

4 garlic cloves, sliced

½ teaspoon red pepper flakes

1 cup dry white wine

6 cups whole-leaf greens, sliced to 3-inch-wide strips (I use escarole)

½ cup extra-virgin olive oil

Kosher salt and freshly ground black pepper

1 cup fresh flat-leaf parsley leaves, roughly chopped

1 Set a large heavy-bottomed skillet over medium-high heat. When the pan is hot, add the clams, tomatoes, garlic, pepper flakes, and wine. Cover and cook until all of the clams have steamed open, about 5 minutes, and discard any that are still closed. Add the greens and olive oil, season with a pinch of salt and a twist of pepper, and cook until the greens have wilted, about 1 minute.

2 Remove from the heat, stir in the parsley, and serve.

ARUGULA SALAD
WITH GRAPES, WALNUTS, AND BLUE CHEESE

SERVES 2

Fresh figs truly are a gift from Mother Nature. Thanks to their inherent sweetness, these tender fruits are often called "nature's candy." You can eat the whole fruit, skin and all, after trimming a bit off the stem end. In this rich, satisfying salad, the figs are combined with blue cheese—a classic pairing—crunchy walnuts, and mildly bitter arugula. This dish makes a great lunch on its own, but also works fantastically as a side or base to grilled meats.

½ cup chopped walnuts

1 tablespoon raw apple cider vinegar

1 teaspoon Dijon mustard

1 teaspoon raw honey

2 tablespoons extra-virgin olive oil

Kosher salt and freshly ground black pepper

4 cups arugula

⅓ cup halved grapes or 6 fresh figs

4 tablespoons crumbled blue cheese

1 Preheat the oven to 350°F.

2 Arrange the walnuts on a sheet pan and cook until lightly toasted, about 8 minutes. Transfer the walnuts to a cutting board and when cool enough to handle, roughly chop and set aside.

3 In a medium bowl, whisk together the vinegar, mustard, honey, and olive oil. Season with a pinch of salt and a twist of pepper. Add the arugula, grapes, walnuts, and blue cheese. Toss to combine and serve.

VIETNAMESE-STYLE STEAK SALAD

SERVES 2

By my estimate, we tested this recipe about twenty times to get the flavors and textures just the way we wanted. It starts with an umami-rich marinade that takes its cues from Vietnamese, Thai, and even Korean kitchens. A little fish sauce goes a long way, but a bottle stays good for years in the fridge, so don't worry if you only pull it out occasionally. In addition to this salad, I like to use this dressing as a base for stir-fries, a marinade for meats bound for the grill, or sneak it into a savory caramel and serve with vegetables, fish, chicken, or pork.

¼ cup tamari (wheat-free soy sauce)

1 teaspoon fish sauce

1 teaspoon light brown sugar

1 garlic clove, minced

1 teaspoon grated fresh ginger

1 (12-ounce) flank steak

2 tablespoons extra-virgin olive oil

Kosher salt and freshly ground black pepper

Juice of 2 limes

4 scallions, thinly sliced

½ cup fresh mint leaves, torn

½ cup fresh cilantro leaves, torn

6 radishes, sliced

1½ cups mung bean sprouts

1 In a medium bowl, whisk together the tamari, fish sauce, brown sugar, garlic, and ginger.

2 Pierce the steak with a fork all over the surface, transfer to a gallon-size zip-top bag, add the marinade, and refrigerate for at least 1 hour and up to 4 hours.

3 Preheat a grill or grill pan to medium-high heat.

4 Remove the steak from the bag, allowing most of the marinade to drip off (discard the marinade).

5 Drizzle the steak on both sides with 1 tablespoon of the olive oil and season with a few pinches of salt and twists of pepper. Put the steak on the grill and cook until nicely charred and medium-rare, about 5 minutes per side. Set aside to rest, loosely tented with foil, for 5 minutes before thinly slicing it against the grain.

6 Meanwhile, in a medium bowl, whisk together the lime juice and remaining 1 tablespoon olive oil. Add the scallions, mint, cilantro, radishes, and bean sprouts and toss to combine.

7 Transfer the salad to a plate, top with sliced steak, and serve.

Dinners

FRIED CHICKEN THIGHS
WITH SPICY CABBAGE AND CARROT SLAW

SERVES 2

Yes, you can be flour-free *and* indulge in fried chicken—and my coating, made with cornstarch, is so crunchy, your next-door neighbors will hear you biting into it! As much as I'd like to, I don't eat fried food every day. So when I do, I want it to really satisfy my craving for crackly, crunchy goodness. This process might seem a little involved, but the shatteringly crisp results are worth it. You can apply the same technique to white meat chicken, fish, or even vegetables, just adjust the fry time accordingly.

2 tablespoons rice vinegar

1 teaspoon grated fresh ginger

1 teaspoon raw honey

1 tablespoon extra-virgin olive oil

Kosher salt and freshly ground black pepper

1 cup thinly sliced red cabbage

½ cup grated carrot

1 small jalapeño, seeded and thinly sliced

1 scallion, thinly sliced

1 In a large bowl, whisk to combine the vinegar, ginger, honey, and olive oil. Season with a pinch of salt and a twist of pepper. Add the cabbage, carrot, jalapeño, and scallion and toss to combine. Add the sesame seeds and refrigerate until needed.

2 In a gallon-size zip-top bag, add ½ cup of the cornstarch, 1 teaspoon of the baking powder, and a pinch of salt and shake to blend. Season both sides of the chicken with a few pinches of salt and twists of pepper. Dredge the chicken thighs in the cornstarch mixture, making sure to coat all sides well. Shake off the excess. Place the chicken on a wire rack set on a sheet pan and refrigerate uncovered at least 2 hours, but up to overnight.

1 tablespoon white sesame seeds

¾ cup cornstarch

1½ teaspoons baking powder

4 boneless, skinless chicken thighs

Peanut oil, for frying

¼ cup rice flour

1 teaspoon turmeric

½ teaspoon smoked paprika

2 tablespoons vodka

3 Pour 4 inches of peanut oil into a deep-fryer or deep heavy-bottomed pot. Set over medium-high heat and heat the oil to 360°F.

4 In a large bowl, combine the rice flour, turmeric, remaining ¼ cup cornstarch, remaining ½ teaspoon baking powder, the paprika, and a pinch of salt and whisk to blend. Add the vodka and ⅓ cup water and stir until no lumps remain. Let stand for 1 minute.

5 When the oil is hot, dip the chicken into the batter and allow the excess to drip off. Carefully add it to the oil and cook until lightly golden brown and crispy, about 6 minutes. Remove using a slotted spoon and drain on a plate lined with paper towels. Season with a few pinches of salt.

6 Serve immediately with the slaw.

CHICKEN PAILLARD
WITH GREEN PAPAYA SALAD

SERVES 2

It might require a special trip to an Asian market, but do try and track down unripe green papaya to make this recipe. Most of us are familiar with ripe, sweet, melon-like papaya, but when picked before it ripens and while still green, papaya has a great crunchy texture that really perks up salads. Green papaya also has a less intense sweetness that pairs beautifully with grilled or roasted meats, fish, and seafood.

2 boneless, skinless chicken breasts (6 ounces each)

1 tablespoon grated fresh ginger

Grated zest of 1 lime

3 tablespoons extra-virgin olive oil

Kosher salt and freshly ground black pepper

Juice of 2 limes

1 tablespoon fish sauce

1 tablespoon light brown sugar

2 cups shredded green papaya or green mango

1 jalapeño, seeded and thinly sliced

¼ cup fresh cilantro, roughly chopped

2 tablespoons unsalted roasted peanuts

1 cup mung bean sprouts

1 Place the chicken breasts on a large sheet of plastic wrap and cover with a second sheet. Use a meat mallet to pound the chicken to an even ½-inch thickness. Place the chicken in a gallon-size zip-top bag.

2 In a medium bowl, whisk together the ginger, lime zest, and 2 tablespoons of the olive oil. Pour the marinade over the chicken and refrigerate for up to 1 hour.

3 Preheat a grill or grill pan to medium-high heat.

4 Remove the chicken from the bag, allowing most of the marinade to drip off (discard the marinade). Season both sides of the chicken with salt and pepper, place on the grill, and cook until nicely charred, about 5 minutes. Flip the chicken and continue cooking until the other side is also nicely charred, about 3 minutes.

5 Meanwhile, in a medium bowl, whisk together the lime juice, fish sauce, brown sugar, and remaining 1 tablespoon olive oil. Add the papaya, jalapeño, cilantro, peanuts, and bean sprouts, season with a pinch of salt and a twist of pepper, and toss to combine.

6 Transfer the salad to plates, slice the chicken, and serve on top of the salads.

HALIBUT IN PEPPER BROTH
WITH CAULIFLOWER AND CARROT

SERVES 1

Poaching fish gently in broth is an almost foolproof way to avoid mistakes like overcooking. Not only does the liquid keep the fish moist, but, when using a flavorful broth like this one, it also adds a ton of depth in the process. The addition of turmeric imparts a lovely golden hue to the flesh of the fish, while providing those famous anti-inflammatory properties. This recipe calls for halibut, one of my favorite types of fish because of its richness, but you can easily substitute other flaky varieties like cod, flounder, or striped bass.

1 red bell pepper, roughly chopped

Juice of 1 lemon

1 teaspoon ground turmeric

Kosher salt and freshly ground black pepper

2 tablespoons extra-virgin olive oil

2 carrots, diced

2 cups cauliflower florets

2 skinless halibut fillets (8 ounces each)

1 cup dry white wine

2 tablespoons finely chopped fresh flat-leaf parsley

1 In a blender or food processor, combine the bell pepper, lemon juice, turmeric, and ¼ teaspoon black pepper and process until mostly smooth. Set aside until needed.

2 Set a large skillet over medium-high heat. Add the olive oil and heat to shimmering, then add the carrots and cauliflower. Season with a pinch of salt and a twist of pepper and cook until the vegetables begin to soften and brown, about 3 minutes.

3 Move the vegetables to the outer edge of the skillet. To the open space in the center, add the halibut and season with a pinch of salt and a twist of pepper. Add the red pepper puree and wine. Reduce the heat to medium-low, cover, and cook until the halibut is cooked through, about 5 minutes. Uncover and baste the fish with the sauce.

4 Transfer the vegetables to a plate and top with the halibut. Stir the parsley into the red pepper puree in the skillet, spoon over fish, and serve.

PORK STIR-FRY
WITH VEGETABLE BROWN RICE

SERVES 2

2 tablespoons extra-virgin olive oil

2 tablespoons toasted sesame oil

1 (12-ounce) pork tenderloin, thinly sliced

Kosher salt and freshly ground black pepper

2 cups shaved Brussels sprouts

2 carrots, shredded on the large holes of a box grater

½ cup raw cashews

2 tablespoons grated fresh ginger

4 garlic cloves, sliced

2 cups cooked rice (I use brown rice)

4 tablespoons rice vinegar

2 tablespoons tamari (wheat-free soy sauce)

½ cup chopped fresh cilantro

After a little bit of prep work, this dish comes together in less than 10 minutes. It's loaded with lean pork tenderloin (which is tender and moist, too) and healthy veggies, layered with bold flavors like fresh ginger and cilantro, crunchy toasted cashews, and blended with cooked rice to create a sort of stir-fry/fried-rice hybrid. Perfect for lunch or dinner, this delicious meal is in my regular rotation. If you want to sub out the pork for white meat chicken breast, sliced portobello mushrooms, or eggplant, it would still be great. As for the brown rice, it, too, can be substituted by leftover cooked quinoa, farro, or white rice.

1 Set a large skillet over medium-high heat. Add the olive oil and sesame oil and heat to shimmering, then add the pork slices in a single layer. Season with a pinch of salt and a twist of pepper and cook, without stirring, until lightly golden brown, about 5 minutes. Flip the pork, add the Brussels sprouts, carrots, and cashews, and continue cooking until the second side is golden brown and the vegetables are tender, about 3 minutes. Add the ginger, garlic, and rice and cook until aromatic, about 2 minutes.

2 Remove from the heat, stir in the vinegar, tamari, and cilantro, and serve.

SHRIMP WITH CORN, COCONUT, AND GLASS NOODLES

SERVES 2

Cellophane noodles, often called glass noodles because of their translucence when cooked, are popular in Asian soups and stir-fries. They have a pleasantly chewy texture and excel at absorbing the flavors around them. In this case, it's the creamy goodness of coconut milk. Combined with the sweet shrimp and bright pops of fresh cilantro, this noodle bowl is as comforting and satisfying as they come.

3 ounces cellophane noodles

2 tablespoons extra-virgin olive oil

10 medium shrimp, peeled and deveined

Kosher salt and freshly ground black pepper

1 cup thinly sliced bell pepper (I use red)

1 jalapeño, seeded and thinly sliced

4 scallions, thinly sliced

4 garlic cloves, thinly sliced

1 cup fresh corn kernels

2 cups unsweetened full-fat coconut milk or other nondairy milk

⅓ cup finely chopped fresh cilantro

1 In a medium bowl, add the cellophane noodles and cover with warm water by a few inches. Allow to soak at room temperature for 10 minutes.

2 Meanwhile, set a large skillet over medium heat. Add the olive oil and heat to shimmering, then add the shrimp in a single layer. Season with a pinch of salt and a twist of pepper and cook until the shrimp turn pink on one side, about 2 minutes. Flip and continue cooking for 1 minute. Transfer the shrimp to a plate and set aside.

3 To the same skillet, add the bell pepper, jalapeño, and a pinch of salt. Cook until the vegetables begin to soften, about 3 minutes. Add the scallions, garlic, corn, a pinch of salt, and a twist of pepper and cook until aromatic, about 2 minutes. Add the coconut milk and bring to a simmer. Drain the cellophane noodles and add to the skillet along with the shrimp. Stir and cook for 1 minute.

4 Remove from the heat, stir in the cilantro, and serve.

SKIRT STEAK WITH PISTACHIO CHIMICHURRI AND CAULIFLOWER "RICE"

SERVES 2

3 tablespoons golden raisins

1 cup riced cauliflower (see page 196)

2 tablespoons salt-packed capers, rinsed

¼ cup roasted pistachios

1 garlic clove, minced

¼ teaspoon ground cumin

¼ teaspoon red pepper flakes

¼ cup finely chopped fresh flat-leaf parsley

¼ cup fresh mint leaves, thinly sliced

Grated zest and juice of 1 orange

1 teaspoon sherry vinegar

¼ cup plus 1 tablespoon extra-virgin olive oil

Kosher salt and freshly ground black pepper

1 (12-ounce) skirt steak, trimmed of silver skin

Here, an herby, salty, citrusy chimichurri is enhanced with heaps of crunchy cauliflower, transforming it into a kind of loose salad. The saucy salad is the perfect foil to the savory grilled steak. You can make the chimichurri a day or two ahead to save time; just store it in an airtight container in the fridge.

1 Set a small saucepan over medium-high heat. Add the raisins and ¼ cup water and bring to a simmer. Remove from the heat and let stand for 5 minutes to rehydrate.

2 Drain the raisins and add them to a large bowl along with the cauliflower, capers, pistachios, garlic, cumin, pepper flakes, parsley, mint, orange zest, orange juice, vinegar, and ¼ cup of the olive oil. Season with a pinch of salt and a twist of pepper and toss to combine.

3 Preheat a grill or grill pan to medium-high heat.

4 Drizzle the steak on both sides with the remaining 1 tablespoon olive oil and season with a few pinches of salt and twists of pepper. Put the steak on the grill and cook until nicely charred and medium-rare, about 3 minutes per side. Set aside to rest, loosely tented with foil, for 5 minutes before thinly slicing it against the grain.

5 Serve the sliced steak topped with the pistachio chimichurri/cauliflower salad.

Snacks

When coming up with these snack recipes, I wanted to create items that would satisfy the desire for something sweet, crunchy, chewy, salty, or all of the above. But I also wanted to keep things wholesome and natural. And obviously, all of them are flour-free. Other than the radishes, which are a fresh, quick-to-assemble treat, the recipes are designed to make enough to have for days or even weeks. The muffins freeze well, requiring just about 5 minutes in a 350°F oven to refresh, while the bark stores well for up to a month in the pantry. Feel free to use any nuts that you like or happen to have in the granola because the recipe is super flexible.

RADISHES WITH TURMERIC-CHILI SALT

SERVES 1

1 tablespoon flaky
sea salt

½ tablespoon grated
fresh turmeric or
½ teaspoon ground
turmeric

½ teaspoon chili powder

½ teaspoon sweet or
smoked paprika

6 radishes, halved

In a medium bowl, combine the salt, turmeric, chili powder, and paprika. Dip the radishes in the seasoned salt for a healthy, crunchy snack. Store any extra turmeric/chili salt in an airtight container indefinitely.

BREAKFAST MUFFINS

MAKES 18 MUFFINS

2 cups almond flour

1½ cups old-fashioned rolled oats

2 teaspoons ground cinnamon

1 teaspoon baking soda

½ teaspoon kosher salt

½ cup chopped pecans

3 large eggs

½ cup raw honey or pure maple syrup

½ cup coconut oil (melted if solid)

Grated zest of 1 orange

1 Granny Smith apple, unpeeled and grated on the large holes of a box grater (discard the core and seeds)

2 carrots, peeled and grated on the large holes of a box grater

1 small zucchini, grated on the large holes of a box grater

1 Preheat the oven to 350°F. Line two 12-cup muffin tins with paper liners.

2 In a large bowl, combine the almond flour, oats, cinnamon, baking soda, salt, and pecans and toss to combine.

3 In a separate large bowl, combine the eggs, honey, coconut oil, and orange zest and whisk to combine. Add the apple, carrots, and zucchini and toss to combine. Transfer the egg mixture to the bowl of dry ingredients and stir until just combined.

4 Divide the mixture evenly among 18 muffin cups, filling each to the rim.

5 Bake until the muffins are nicely browned on top and a knife inserted into the center comes out clean, about 25 minutes. Allow to cool completely before storing in an airtight container for up to 3 days in the fridge or 2 weeks in the freezer.

GRANOLA BARK

MAKES 2 POUNDS

3 cups old-fashioned rolled oats

1 cup roughly chopped almonds

1 cup unsweetened shredded coconut

½ cup chia seeds

½ cup flax meal

¼ cup sesame seeds

½ cup almond flour

2 teaspoons ground cinnamon

1 teaspoon kosher salt

2 large egg whites

2 teaspoons vanilla extract

½ cup raw honey or pure maple syrup

⅓ cup extra-virgin olive oil

1 Preheat the oven to 325°F. Line a sheet pan with parchment paper.

2 In a large bowl, combine the oats, chopped almonds, coconut, chia seeds, flax meal, sesame seeds, almond flour, cinnamon, and salt and toss to combine.

3 In a medium bowl, whisk the egg whites until thin and frothy, about 1 minute. Whisk in the vanilla. Transfer the egg whites to the granola mixture along with the honey and olive oil. Stir well to combine, then transfer to the lined sheet pan. Spread the mixture into an even layer on the parchment paper. Top with a second piece of parchment paper. Place a second sheet pan on top of the parchment paper and press to form a nice even layer. Remove the second sheet pan and top piece of parchment paper before baking.

4 Bake until golden brown and crisp, about 45 minutes. Remove from the oven and allow to cool completely in the pan before breaking it into pieces. Store in an airtight container for up to 2 weeks.

NO MEAT

Breakfasts

Baked Eggs in Creamy
Spinach **176**

Breakfast Panzanella
(as seen above) **179**

Veggie Frittata Muffins **180**

Baked Oatmeal with
Blackberries and Almonds **183**

Mission-Style
Breakfast Burritos **184**

Pomodoro Baked Eggs
with Parmesan and Basil **187**

Crostini with Scrambled Eggs
and Salsa **188**

Lunches

Cauliflower and
Chickpea Curry **189**

Mushroom Udon Soup
(as seen above) **192**

Farro with Corn, Parsley,
and Peppers **195**

Kimchi Cauliflower
Fried "Rice" **196**

Broccoli Chowder **199**

Spaghetti Squash
Pancakes **200**

Lentil and Swiss
Chard Soup **203**

Dinners

Snacks

Breakfasts

BAKED EGGS IN CREAMY SPINACH

SERVES 2

I've come up with a million different variations on the shakshuka theme, which essentially is a hearty skillet of eggs simmered in a robustly flavored base. These one-pan wonders offer the oozy richness of poached eggs without all the fuss. In this version, creamy, cheesy, nutrient-dense spinach serves as the base for the eggs, but you can just as easily use equally wholesome Swiss chard, kale, or collard greens. Also, a couple shakes of hot sauce is never a bad idea. Serve this savory and satisfying dish with grilled or toasted bread.

2 tablespoons extra-virgin olive oil

½ cup finely chopped onion

Kosher salt and freshly ground black pepper

4 cups sliced spinach leaves

1 cup heavy cream

½ teaspoon freshly grated nutmeg

4 tablespoons freshly grated parmesan cheese

4 large eggs

1 Preheat the oven to 350°F.

2 Set a large ovenproof skillet over medium-high heat. Add the olive oil and heat to shimmering, then add the onion and a pinch of salt. Cook until translucent, about 1 minute. Add the spinach and cook until wilted, about 1 minute. Add the cream and bring to a simmer. Add the nutmeg and parmesan and season with a pinch of salt and a twist of pepper.

3 Make 4 shallow depressions in the spinach mixture and carefully crack an egg into each one. Transfer the skillet to the oven and cook until the egg whites are set but the yolks are still runny, about 8 minutes. Serve immediately.

BREAKFAST PANZANELLA

SERVES 2

Here we turn panzanella (page 113) into a savory breakfast with the addition of poached eggs. The magic happens when you slice into an egg, releasing the warm, oozy yolks onto the crispy-crunchy, crouton-like toasts. That yolk also enriches the vinaigrette.

3 tablespoons extra-virgin olive oil

1 garlic clove, minced

1 tablespoon freshly grated parmesan cheese, plus more for serving

2 cups cubed (½-inch) rustic bread

Kosher salt and freshly ground black pepper

1 tablespoon red wine vinegar

1 teaspoon Dijon mustard

1 medium tomato, quartered

2 tablespoons white wine vinegar

4 large eggs

½ cup chopped fresh basil

¼ cup thinly sliced red onion

1 Preheat the oven to 350°F. Line a sheet pan with foil.

2 In a medium bowl, whisk together 2 tablespoons of the olive oil, the garlic, and parmesan. Add the bread cubes, season with salt and pepper, and toss to coat. Arrange in a single layer on the sheet pan and cook until lightly golden brown and crisp, about 12 minutes.

3 In the same bowl, whisk to combine the red wine vinegar, mustard, and remaining 1 tablespoon olive oil. Roughly chop one of the tomato quarters and crush it into the vinaigrette using your hands. Season with salt and pepper.

4 In a medium saucepan, combine 4 cups water and the white wine vinegar and bring to a strong simmer over medium-high heat. Crack each egg into its own little bowl. With a spoon, create a large (but gentle) whirlpool in the simmering water by stirring in one direction around the perimeter of the pan. Gently lower the eggs into the center of the pan. Poach, untouched, until each egg is set enough to be lifted out of the water without breaking but the yolk is still runny, about 3 minutes. Use a slotted spoon to gently transfer to a paper towel.

5 Transfer the toasted bread to the bowl with the vinaigrette. Add the basil, red onion, and remaining tomato quarters, season with salt and pepper, and toss to combine.

6 Divide the panzanella between two bowls, top each with 2 eggs, garnish with parmesan, and serve.

VEGGIE FRITTATA MUFFINS

MAKES 12 MUFFINS

Baking these frittatas in a muffin tin removes a lot of the anxiety that comes with larger skillet versions, which require a good bit of finesse to remove from the pan. The convenient size of these "mini-frits" also makes them extremely portable, so they can easily be popped into a backpack or purse and enjoyed as a snack any time, any place. They also freeze incredibly well, requiring just 3 to 5 minutes in a 350°F oven to come back to life. Sliced, diced, and shredded zucchini, carrot, or yellow squash all would be great swaps for the bell pepper.

2 tablespoons extra-virgin olive oil

¼ cup thinly sliced scallions

½ cup diced red bell pepper

1 cup thinly sliced spinach leaves

8 large eggs

½ cup heavy cream

Kosher salt and freshly ground black pepper

1 cup shredded cheddar cheese

1 Preheat the oven to 350°F. Grease 12 cups of a muffin tin with the olive oil.

2 Evenly divide the scallions, bell pepper, and spinach among the muffin cups.

3 In a large bowl, whisk to blend the eggs, cream, a pinch of salt, and a twist of pepper. Divide the egg mixture evenly among the muffin cups. Divide the cheddar evenly among the muffin cups.

4 Bake until lightly golden brown and puffy, about 30 minutes.

5 Let the frittata muffins stand for 5 minutes before serving. Leftover muffins will last up to 5 days in the fridge and up to 1 month in the freezer.

BAKED OATMEAL
WITH BLACKBERRIES AND ALMONDS

SERVES 2

If you're only used to stovetop oatmeal, this recipe is going to change your life! Not only is baked oatmeal more of a hands-off affair, but the end product is a million times more satisfying, in my opinion. You end up with a warm, slightly sweet oatmeal casserole that gets a big protein boost from the eggs. And of course the oats bring with them all that whole-grain goodness, including heaps of soluble fiber as well as antioxidant and anti-inflammatory properties. Feel free to swap in different fruits, nuts, and even milks—the possibilities are endless!

¼ cup sliced or slivered almonds

1 cup blackberries

1 cup old-fashioned rolled oats

½ teaspoon ground cinnamon

Kosher salt

2 large eggs

⅔ cup unsweetened almond milk or other nondairy milk

1 teaspoon vanilla extract

2 tablespoons pure maple syrup

1 Preheat the oven to 350°F.

2 Arrange the almonds on a sheet pan and cook until lightly toasted, about 8 minutes. Set aside. Leave the oven on.

3 Scatter the blackberries in the bottom of a small ovenproof baking dish (I use a 5 × 8-inch baking dish). Top with the oats, cinnamon, and a pinch of salt.

4 In a small bowl, whisk together the eggs, milk, vanilla, and maple syrup. Pour over the oats.

5 Transfer to the oven and bake until set, about 20 minutes.

6 Serve topped with the toasted almonds.

MISSION-STYLE BREAKFAST BURRITOS

SERVES 2

I call these "Mission-style" because, like the original West Coast burritos, these are big, burly, and jam-packed with flavor and texture. What can be better than a healthy, satisfying breakfast burrito stuffed with creamy avocado, melty cheese, and gently cooked scrambled eggs? One that gets crisped up in a hot skillet, that's what. Don't sleep on the fresh avocado because it's packed with potassium and also the "good" kind of fat that fights the "bad" kind of cholesterol.

2 (10-inch) whole wheat tortillas

1 cup shredded Monterey Jack cheese

½ cup diced tomato

½ avocado, sliced

2 tablespoons finely chopped fresh cilantro

1½ tablespoons extra-virgin olive oil

1 jalapeño, seeded and finely chopped

2 scallions, thinly sliced

Kosher salt and freshly ground black pepper

6 large eggs

1 Dividing evenly, fill in the bottom third of the tortillas with the cheese, tomato, avocado, and cilantro and set aside.

2 Set a large nonstick skillet over medium-low heat. Add 1 tablespoon of the olive oil followed by the jalapeño, scallions, and a pinch of salt. Cook for 1 minute.

3 In a medium bowl, whisk together the eggs, a pinch of salt, and a twist of pepper to thoroughly blend. Pour the eggs into the skillet and cook, stirring constantly, until small, soft curds form, about 3 minutes.

4 Add half the scrambled eggs to one tortilla. Fold the bottom of the wrapper in over the filling a bit, then fold the two sides in over the filling, and give the roll one turn forward to form a burrito. Repeat with remaining eggs and tortilla to make a second burrito.

5 Wipe out the skillet, set over medium heat, and add the remaining ½ tablespoon olive oil. Add the burritos seam-side down and cook until golden brown and crisp on one side, about 1 minute. Flip and continue cooking until the other side is lightly browned, about 30 seconds.

6 Slice the burritos in half and serve.

POMODORO BAKED EGGS
WITH PARMESAN AND BASIL

SERVES 2

This is a variation on the popular dish often referred to as Eggs in Purgatory, in which eggs are poached in a spicy—and well-spiced—tomato sauce. To me, these recipes are so flexible and forgiving that I keep going back to them. Sauté some greens like spinach, Swiss chard, or kale with the aromatic vegetables if you want, swap the pepper flakes for sliced fresh jalapeño, or finish the dish with any soft green herb like cilantro, parsley, or tarragon. This type of recipe also doubles with ease, making it a great brunch recipe.

Small bunch of fresh oregano

Small bunch of fresh thyme

2 tablespoons extra-virgin olive oil

½ small yellow onion, diced

2 garlic cloves, sliced

Kosher salt and freshly ground black pepper

¼ teaspoon red pepper flakes

1 (15-ounce) can crushed San Marzano tomatoes

4 large eggs

¼ cup thinly sliced fresh basil

1 tablespoon freshly grated parmesan cheese

1 Preheat the oven to 350°F.

2 Bundle up the oregano and thyme in butcher's twine and set aside.

3 Set a large ovenproof heavy-bottomed skillet over medium-low heat. Add the olive oil followed by the onion, garlic, and a pinch of salt. Cook, stirring occasionally, until the vegetables soften, about 5 minutes. Add the pepper flakes, tomatoes, and the herb bundle. Season with a pinch of salt and a twist of pepper. Bring to a simmer and cook uncovered for 15 minutes. Discard the herb bundle.

4 Carefully crack the eggs into the sauce, transfer the skillet to the oven, and cook until the egg whites are set but the yolks are still runny, about 8 minutes.

5 Top with the basil and parmesan and serve from the skillet.

CROSTINI WITH SCRAMBLED EGGS AND SALSA

SERVES 2

Simple, satisfying, and impressive, crostini never fail to hit the mark. The interplay of textures that results from the soft scrambled eggs atop the crispy grilled toasts is the main selling point, so skip the bland sandwich bread and go rustic! If you enjoy a little wake-up spice, add a dash of red pepper flakes to the scrambled eggs before cooking them.

1 large tomato, diced

2 scallions, thinly sliced

1 garlic clove, minced

4 tablespoons sliced fresh basil leaves

4 tablespoons extra-virgin olive oil

Kosher salt and freshly ground black pepper

4 (1-inch-thick) slices rustic bread

6 large eggs

1 In a medium bowl, combine the tomato, scallions, garlic, basil, and 2 tablespoons of the olive oil. Season with a pinch of salt and a twist of pepper and toss to combine.

2 Preheat a grill or grill pan to medium-high heat.

3 Drizzle both sides of the bread with 1 tablespoon of the olive oil and season with a few pinches of salt and twists of pepper. Put the bread on the grill and cook until nicely charred, about 30 seconds per side. Remove from the grill and set aside.

4 In a large nonstick skillet, heat the remaining 1 tablespoon olive oil over medium-low heat. In a medium bowl, whisk together the eggs, a pinch of salt, and a twist of pepper to thoroughly blend. Pour the eggs into the skillet and cook, stirring constantly, until small, soft curds form, about 3 minutes.

5 Spoon the scrambled eggs onto the grilled bread, top with the tomato mixture, and serve.

Lunches

CAULIFLOWER AND CHICKPEA CURRY

SERVES 2

Here is a recipe that smells as good as it tastes. The red curry sauce fills the kitchen with warm, comforting aromas. It's like walking into a bustling spice bazaar! In addition to all the great smells and flavors, this dish benefits from amazing textures—from the crunchy cashews to the creamy chickpeas. Those humble chickpeas, by the way, are a great source of protein, soluble fiber, and key nutrients. If you like your eggs runny like I do, the oozing yolks add another level of richness to this amazing meal.

1 tablespoon Thai red curry paste, store-bought or homemade (see page 121)

Juice of 1 lime

4 tablespoons raw cashews

Kosher salt and freshly ground black pepper

4 tablespoons extra-virgin olive oil, plus more as needed

2 cups small cauliflower florets

1 jalapeño, seeded and finely chopped

1 In a medium saucepan, whisk to combine 1¼ cups water, the curry paste, and lime juice. Add 2 tablespoons of the cashews and a pinch of salt and bring to a boil over medium-high heat. Reduce to a simmer and cook until the cashews soften, about 15 minutes. Transfer the mixture to a blender or food processor and process until smooth.

2 Set a large skillet over medium-high heat. Add 2 tablespoons of the olive oil and heat to shimmering, then add the cauliflower and a pinch of salt. Cook until the cauliflower begins to soften and brown, about 5 minutes. Stir in the remaining 2 tablespoons cashews, the jalapeño, garlic, and ginger and continue cooking until aromatic, about 3 minutes. If the pan appears dry, add 1 tablespoon olive oil. Add ½ cup water, the chickpeas, and curry-

(recipe and ingredients continue)

1 garlic clove, minced

½ teaspoon grated fresh ginger

½ cup cooked or canned chickpeas (drained and rinsed if using canned)

1 tablespoon whole-milk Greek yogurt

1 tablespoon finely chopped fresh cilantro

2 large eggs

cashew puree and bring to a simmer. Taste and adjust for seasoning, adding salt and pepper as needed. Remove from the heat and stir in the yogurt and cilantro. Cover and keep warm until needed.

3 Set a large nonstick skillet over medium heat. Add the remaining 1 tablespoon olive oil and heat to shimmering. Carefully crack the eggs into the pan and cook until the whites begin to brown around the edges, about 2 minutes. Season with a pinch of salt and a twist of pepper. Remove from the heat, add 1 tablespoon water, cover, and let steam for 30 seconds for runny yolks, 1 minute for medium-set yolks, and 1½ minutes for fully set yolks.

4 Divide the cauliflower and chickpea curry between two plates, top each with an egg, and serve.

MUSHROOM UDON SOUP

SERVES 2

Liz calls this dish "a giant bowl of happiness" and I totally agree! When you have great stock (like Mushroom Broth, page 249) on hand in the freezer, an amazing meal like this one can come together in no time at all—that said, even if you use store-bought broth, this is a quick-to-make, hearty, healthy meal. Fat, chewy udon noodles made from wheat really up the comfort factor of this soup, but if you can't find them, go ahead and use fresh or dried ramen noodles or even spaghetti. It will still be delicious and nutritious thanks to the restorative magic of mushrooms, ginger, and kale.

Kosher salt and freshly ground black pepper

3½ ounces udon noodles

2 tablespoons extra-virgin olive oil

1 cup sliced cremini mushrooms

2 scallions, thinly sliced

1 tablespoon grated fresh ginger

2 cups sliced kale leaves and tender stems

2 cups Mushroom Broth (page 249)

2 teaspoons tamari (wheat-free soy sauce)

1 Fill a medium saucepan with water and a big pinch of salt and bring to a boil over high heat. Add the udon noodles and cook until tender, about 4 minutes. Drain, rinse under cold water, and set aside.

2 Return the saucepan to medium heat. Add the oil and heat to shimmering, then add the mushrooms. Cook, without stirring, until they begin to brown and crisp on one side, about 3 minutes. Add the scallions, ginger, and kale, season with a pinch of salt and a twist of black pepper, and continue cooking until the kale has wilted, about 2 minutes. Add the mushroom broth and tamari, bring to a simmer, and cook for 5 minutes.

3 Divide the udon noodles between two bowls, top with the mushroom and kale broth, and serve.

FARRO WITH CORN, PARSLEY, AND PEPPERS

SERVES 2

Farro is whole-grain goodness! This so-called ancient grain has a pleasantly chewy texture, compelling nutty flavor, and it's super healthy. Pound for pound, it packs more protein, fiber, and nutrients than almost any other grain. It also plays well with almost any vegetable, making it a useful base for recipes all year long. In summer, I pair it with corn, parsley, and bell pepper as in this recipe, but in fall and winter I reach for hearty root veggies like roasted carrots, beets, and sweet potatoes.

½ cup farro

1½ cups Mushroom Broth (page 249)

Kosher salt and freshly ground black pepper

4 tablespoons extra-virgin olive oil

½ cup fresh corn kernels

½ red bell pepper, diced

2 tablespoons chopped fresh flat-leaf parsley

Juice of ½ lemon

1 Set a small saucepan over medium heat and add the farro, mushroom broth, and a pinch of salt. Bring to a boil and then reduce the heat to medium-low to maintain a gentle simmer. Cook, partially covered, until the farro is tender but still a little chewy, about 20 minutes. Remove from the heat and let stand for 5 minutes.

2 Set a large skillet over medium heat. Add 2 tablespoons of the olive oil and heat to shimmering, then add the corn and bell pepper. Season with a pinch of salt and a twist of pepper and cook until the vegetables soften, about 3 minutes.

3 In a medium bowl, combine the farro, cooked vegetables, remaining 2 tablespoons olive oil, the parsley, and lemon juice and toss to combine. Serve.

KIMCHI CAULIFLOWER FRIED "RICE"

SERVES 2

There aren't many foods that pack as much punch as kimchi. Like many fermented foods, kimchi, a Korean dish typically made from napa cabbage, combines a pleasant tanginess with the amazing health benefits of probiotics. But unlike other popular fermented foods such as sauerkraut and pickles, kimchi is typically aggressively spiced, which is a bonus to heat-lovers. We double down on healthy choices here by swapping out the usual white rice for finely grated cauliflower, which adds great texture along with all those nutrients. If you can't chase down any kimchi, this recipe would work fine with sauerkraut, just add some red pepper flakes, jalapeño, or hot sauce if you like things spicy.

2 tablespoons toasted sesame oil

4 cups riced cauliflower (see below)

½ cup finely diced carrots

½ cup fresh or frozen peas

4 garlic cloves, sliced

Kosher salt and freshly ground black pepper

2 scallions, thinly sliced

2 teaspoons tamari (wheat-free soy sauce)

2 teaspoons oyster sauce

½ cup roughly chopped kimchi

2 large eggs, beaten

1 Set a large skillet over medium-high heat. Add the sesame oil and heat to shimmering, then add the cauliflower, carrots, peas, and garlic. Season with a pinch of salt and a twist of pepper and cook until the vegetables begin to soften and brown, about 3 minutes. Add the scallions, tamari, oyster sauce, and kimchi and cook, stirring occasionally, for 1 minute. Move the vegetables to the outer edge of the pan.

2 To the open space in the middle of the skillet, add the beaten eggs. Cook, stirring constantly, until small, soft curds form, about 2 minutes. Remove from the heat, stir to combine, and serve.

TURNING CAULIFLOWER INTO "RICE"

To make cauliflower rice, grate the florets and tender stems on the large holes of a box grater. Alternatively, place the florets and tender stems in a blender or food processor and pulse until the texture resembles coarse rice.

BROCCOLI CHOWDER

SERVES 2

1 tablespoon plus
1 teaspoon extra-virgin
olive oil

1 tablespoon unsalted
butter

½ medium yellow onion,
finely chopped

2 garlic cloves, sliced

1 jalapeño, seeded and
finely chopped

Kosher salt and freshly
ground black pepper

⅛ teaspoon freshly
grated nutmeg

1 tablespoon thyme
leaves, roughly chopped

1 tablespoon all-purpose
flour

2 cups whole milk

2 small Yukon Gold
potatoes, peeled
and diced

1 cup chopped broccoli
florets and tender stems

½ teaspoon smoky hot
sauce, such as Tabasco
chipotle pepper sauce

Even though I knew it was a sneaky ploy to get me to eat my veggies as a kid, broccoli chowder has always been one of my favorite soups. It still is, even if the versions I make now are a little more "grown-up." In place of a thick and cheesy porridge-like puree of mushy vegetables, this recipe stars oven-roasted broccoli that holds its shape and texture. By starting with a basic béchamel, we achieve a creamy texture without the need for heaps of cheese. A little bit of spice makes everything nice, so don't forget the jalapeño and a few shakes of hot sauce.

1 Preheat the oven to 375°F. Line a sheet pan with foil.

2 Set a medium saucepan over medium heat. Add 1 tablespoon of the olive oil and the butter and heat until melted, then add the onion, garlic, jalapeño, and a pinch of salt. Cook, stirring occasionally, until the vegetables soften, about 3 minutes. Add the nutmeg, thyme, and flour and cook for 30 seconds. While continuously whisking, add the milk. Bring to a simmer and season with a pinch of salt and a twist of pepper. Add the potatoes and cook, stirring occasionally, until the potatoes are soft, about 20 minutes.

3 Meanwhile, arrange the broccoli in an even layer on the sheet pan. Drizzle with the remaining 1 teaspoon olive oil and season with a pinch of salt and a twist of pepper. Cook until the broccoli softens and browns around the edges, about 15 minutes.

4 Carefully transfer the roasted broccoli to the saucepan and stir to combine. Add a few dashes of your favorite smoky hot sauce and serve.

SPAGHETTI SQUASH PANCAKES

SERVES 2

I'm always looking for new and different ways to use spaghetti squash because it's such a versatile and healthy ingredient that boasts high levels of antioxidants like beta-carotene and vitamin C. In this recipe, instead of using it as a carb-free substitute for spaghetti—as it so often is—I use it as the base for crispy, golden-bottomed pancakes. The feta adds a nice salty kick, while the mint, dill, and lemon add summery brightness. This dish is also a great way to use up leftover cooked spaghetti squash. If you want to go gluten-free, you can omit the flour.

1 small spaghetti squash, halved lengthwise, strings and seeds discarded

2 garlic cloves, minced

2 tablespoons finely chopped fresh mint

2 tablespoons finely chopped fresh dill

2 scallions, thinly sliced

Grated zest of 1 lemon

2 large eggs, beaten

¼ cup all-purpose flour (optional)

Kosher salt and freshly ground black pepper

½ cup crumbled feta cheese (optional)

2 tablespoons extra-virgin olive oil

2 tablespoons whole-milk Greek yogurt, for serving (optional)

1 Preheat the oven to 375°F.

2 Set the squash cut-side down in a 9 × 13-inch baking dish. Add ½ cup water to the pan, cover with foil, and cook until the squash is just tender, about 35 minutes. Remove from the oven, discard the foil, and carefully flip the squash (steam will escape). Set aside until cool enough to handle.

3 While still warm, use a fork to scrape the squash flesh into spaghetti-like strands into a large bowl. Add the garlic, mint, dill, scallions, lemon zest, eggs, and flour (if using). Season with a few pinches of salt and twists of pepper and stir to combine. Gently fold in the feta (if using).

4 Set a large nonstick skillet over medium-high heat. Add 1 tablespoon of the olive oil and heat to shimmering, then add the half of the squash mixture to the pan. Smooth it out to an even layer with a spatula and cook, without stirring, until lightly golden brown on the bottom, about 3 minutes. Flip and continue cooking until the other side has browned, about 3 minutes. Transfer to a plate and loosely tent with foil to keep warm while you repeat the process with the remaining 1 tablespoon olive oil and squash mixture.

5 Serve hot. If desired, top the pancakes with yogurt.

LENTIL AND SWISS CHARD SOUP

SERVES 2

My pap was famous in our family for his lentil and split pea soups. Of course, that might have been because they were essentially pork stews embellished with a few handfuls of lentils or peas! There's no meaty ham hock in this recipe, so I'm not going to claim that it's "just as good as Pap's," but the addition of smoked paprika does impart a satisfyingly "meaty," savory undertone. Another chef's tip: Adding a splash or two of vinegar to pea or lentil soups makes a world of difference. The acid awakens the palate like salt, while cutting through the heaviness. If you don't have sherry vinegar on hand, red or white wine vinegar would be great swaps.

1 tablespoon extra-virgin olive oil

½ cup finely diced yellow onion

¼ cup finely diced celery

¼ cup sliced carrot

2 cloves garlic, minced

Kosher salt and freshly ground black pepper

1 potato, such as Yukon Gold, medium-diced

¼ cup green or brown lentils, rinsed

½ teaspoon smoked paprika

½ cup sliced Swiss chard leaves, bottom stems removed

½ teaspoon sherry vinegar

1 Set a large saucepan over medium heat. Add the olive oil and heat to shimmering, then add the onion, celery, carrot, and garlic. Season with a pinch of salt and a twist of pepper. Cook, stirring occasionally, until the vegetables begin to soften, about 3 minutes.

2 Add 2 cups water, the potato, lentils, and smoked paprika and bring to a simmer. Season with a pinch of salt and a twist of black pepper. Cook, partially covered, until the lentils are very soft, about 40 minutes.

3 Remove from the heat, stir in the Swiss chard and vinegar, and serve.

Dinners

RIGATONI WITH ARUGULA, PARSLEY PESTO, AND SUN-DRIED TOMATOES

SERVES 2

If you're bored with basil pesto—or just feel like trying something different—this recipe is for you. I swap the mellow mintiness of fresh basil for the pleasant pepperiness of arugula and parsley, which helps to offset the natural sweetness of the sun-dried tomatoes). Feel free to experiment with different soft herbs to enhance the kale like mint, cilantro, and chives. Same goes for the nuts. I prefer walnuts, but sunflower seeds, almonds, macadamia nuts, and pine nuts all work great.

Kosher salt

½ pound rigatoni

2 cups arugula

½ cup roughly chopped parsley leaves and tender stems

1 garlic clove, sliced

¼ cup walnuts, roughly chopped

¼ cup freshly grated parmesan cheese

½ cup extra-virgin olive oil

⅓ cup oil-packed sun-dried tomatoes, thinly sliced, plus 1 tablespoon oil from the jar

1 Add 3 tablespoons salt to a large pot of water and bring to a boil over high heat. Add the pasta and cook until just al dente, about 2 minutes less than the package directions. Occasionally give the pasta a stir so it doesn't stick together. Scoop out and reserve ½ cup of the pasta water before draining the pasta and returning it to the pot.

2 Meanwhile, in a blender or food processor, combine the arugula, parsley, garlic, walnuts, and parmesan and pulse until the mixture has the consistency of fine bread crumbs. With the machine running, slowly add the olive oil in a steady stream.

3 Transfer the pesto to the pot of pasta, add the reserved pasta water, and stir to combine. Stir in the sun-dried tomatoes and oil from the jar and serve.

CAULIFLOWER CACIO E PEPE

SERVES 2

Cacio e pepe deliciously demonstrates how a few basic ingredients can combine to become so much more than the sum of their parts. *Cacio e pepe* translates to "cheese and pepper"—and this super-popular dish is basically just that, bound together with a little water to create a silky sauce. Now, I know dairy and me don't always agree, but this recipe manages to squeak by with just a handful of aged cheese. Here, we apply that delicious combination in a sauce for roasted cauliflower instead of the customary pasta, but this would be just as good on roasted broccoli, asparagus, or zucchini.

1 medium head cauliflower

4 tablespoons extra-virgin olive oil

Kosher salt and freshly ground black pepper

4 tablespoons unsalted butter

1 cup freshly grated pecorino cheese

1 Preheat the oven to 450°F. Line a sheet pan with foil.

2 To prepare the cauliflower, remove the leaves and all but 1 inch of stem from the head. Place the head stem-side down on the cutting board. With a heavy, sharp knife, slice through the middle of the head to create two equal halves.

3 Drizzle the cauliflower on all sides with 2 tablespoons of the olive oil and arrange cut-side down on the sheet pan. Season with a few pinches of salt and twists of pepper.

4 Roast until golden brown, about 30 minutes. Flip the cauliflower and continue cooking for 15 minutes.

5 Meanwhile, set a medium saucepan over medium heat. Add ¼ cup water and 1 teaspoon black pepper and bring to a simmer. Add the butter and whisk to combine. Remove from the heat and whisk in the pecorino and remaining 2 tablespoons olive oil.

6 Top the cauliflower with the cheese sauce and serve.

VEGETABLE AND PEANUT STIR-FRY

SERVES 2

Juice of 1 lime

1 tablespoon mirin

1 tablespoon tamari
(wheat-free soy sauce)

2 tablespoons toasted
sesame oil

2 medium carrots, thinly
sliced

2 cups sliced mushrooms
(I use cremini)

1 small yellow onion,
sliced

2 garlic cloves, sliced

1 tablespoon grated fresh
ginger

½ teaspoon red pepper
flakes

¼ cup unsalted roasted
peanuts

4 cups ½-inch-thick sliced
napa cabbage

Kosher salt and freshly
ground black pepper

½ cup mung bean sprouts

2 tablespoons finely
chopped fresh cilantro

You don't need a fancy wok to make amazing stir-fries. And once you have this basic technique down, the possibilities are literally endless. Any vegetable is fair game; the key is to have everything cut small and ready to go before you blast the heat. We don't often think of stir-frying cabbage, but it's one of my favorites because it cooks up fast and brings great crisp-tender texture to the party. Plus, cabbage seems to last forever in the fridge, which makes it a great option for when you've all but depleted the veggie bins. Obviously, this dish would be great with steamed white or brown rice, but it's also excellent alongside fluffy couscous or nutty farro.

1 In a small bowl, whisk together the lime juice, mirin, and tamari.

2 Set a large skillet over medium-high heat. Add the sesame oil and heat to shimmering, then add the carrots and mushrooms. Cook until the vegetables begin to soften and brown, about 5 minutes. Add the onion, garlic, ginger, pepper flakes, and peanuts and cook until aromatic, about 3 minutes. Add the cabbage, season with a pinch of salt and a twist of pepper, and cook until the cabbage begins to soften and wilt, about 3 minutes. Add the bean sprouts and tamari mixture and stir to combine.

3 Remove from the heat, stir in the cilantro, and serve.

BAKED ZITI WITH CAULIFLOWER CREAM AND GRUYÈRE

SERVES 2

This dish puts regular macaroni and cheese to shame. Don't let the cauliflower fool you; this is a rich, creamy, and indulgent dish that might require a nap soon after the meal. Thanks to the cauliflower, which adds remarkable body and heft to the sauce, we can get away with using half the dairy of comparable recipes. The Gruyère gives the pasta an elegant, nutty flavor, and the caramelized onions add an earthy-sweet complexity. But the best part might be the golden-brown panko topping. If you don't have ziti on hand, sub in penne or rigatoni.

Kosher salt and freshly ground black pepper

½ pound ziti

5 tablespoons extra-virgin olive oil

4 cups roughly chopped cauliflower

2 garlic cloves, minced

1 tablespoon finely chopped fresh rosemary

½ teaspoon red pepper flakes

2 cups heavy cream

½ cup mascarpone cheese

1 medium yellow onion, sliced

½ cup shredded Gruyère cheese

1 Preheat the oven to 375°F.

2 Add 3 tablespoons salt to a large pot of water and bring to a boil over high heat. Add the pasta and cook until not quite al dente, about 2 minutes less than the package directions. Occasionally give the pasta a stir so it doesn't stick together. Drain, rinse, and set aside.

3 Set a large ovenproof skillet over medium-high heat. Add 3 tablespoons of the olive oil and heat to shimmering, then add the cauliflower. Season with a pinch of salt and a twist of pepper. Cook until the cauliflower begins to soften and brown, about 5 minutes. Add the garlic, rosemary, and pepper flakes and cook for 30 seconds. Add the cream, bring to a simmer, and cook until the cauliflower is soft throughout and the sauce has reduced slightly, about 10 minutes.

4 Carefully transfer the mixture to a blender or food processer. Add the mascarpone and process until smooth. Return the sauce to the skillet, add the drained pasta, stir, and set aside.

½ cup panko bread crumbs

1 tablespoon thinly sliced fresh chives

5 Set another large skillet over medium heat. Add the remaining 2 tablespoons olive oil and heat to shimmering, then add the onion and a pinch of salt. Cook, stirring occasionally, until the onions have deeply caramelized, about 8 minutes. Transfer the onions to the pasta, add the Gruyère, and stir to blend.

6 Top with the panko and bake, uncovered, until golden brown and bubbling, about 45 minutes.

7 Serve garnished with the chives.

ZUCCHINI AND KALE CHOW MEIN

SERVES 2

3 tablespoons tamari (wheat-free soy sauce)

2 teaspoons toasted sesame oil

½ teaspoon cornstarch

1 teaspoon raw honey

3 tablespoons mirin

1 tablespoon grated fresh ginger

2 garlic cloves, minced

Kosher salt and freshly ground black pepper

4 ounces chow mein noodles or Chinese egg noodles

2 tablespoons peanut oil

2 carrots, thinly sliced

1 zucchini, halved lengthwise and thinly sliced crosswise

1 jalapeño, halved, seeded, and thinly sliced

1 red bell pepper, thinly sliced

4 scallions, cut into 2-inch lengths

4 cups greens, sliced into ½-inch wide ribbons (I use kale)

1 cup mung bean sprouts

1 tablespoon toasted sesame seeds

When I was a kid, chow mein noodles meant those crunchy-fried strands that came with stir-fries at the local Chinese restaurant. Now I know (and love) them for what they really are: bouncy egg-based noodles that are sold fresh, frozen, or dried at Asian markets and, increasingly, conventional grocery stores. They are a great addition to stir-fries because they are hardy enough to stand up to bold sauces and heaps of veggies. If your grocer doesn't carry them, look for lo mein noodles. This recipe calls for 4 cups of greens, which might look like a ton but will cook down to almost nothing!

1 In a small bowl, whisk together the tamari, sesame oil, cornstarch, honey, mirin, ginger, garlic, and 2 tablespoons water. Set aside.

2 Add 3 tablespoons salt to a large pot of water and bring to a boil over high heat. Add the pasta and cook according to the package directions. Occasionally give the pasta a stir so it doesn't stick together. Drain, rinse, and set aside.

3 Set a large skillet or wok over medium-high heat. Add the peanut oil and heat to shimmering, then add the carrots and zucchini. Cook until the vegetables begin to soften and brown, about 5 minutes. Add the jalapeño, bell pepper, and scallions. Season with a pinch of salt and a twist of pepper. Cook, stirring occasionally, until the vegetables begin to brown, about 5 minutes. Add the greens and cook until wilted, about 3 minutes. Stir in the cooked noodles, bean sprouts, and tamari mixture.

4 Serve garnished with the sesame seeds.

CRISPY HALLOUMI
WITH ZUCCHINI, TOMATO, AND WALNUTS

SERVES 2

Growing up, we always called Halloumi the "squeaky cheese" because of the way it felt in the mouth. It's a bit rubbery, to be honest, but its firm texture and high melting point are what make the cheese perfect for grilling, sautéing, or frying because it holds its shape. For this dinner, we pair the warm, salty pan-seared cheese with a light, bright, and fresh vegetable salad for the perfect balance.

¼ cup walnuts

2 tablespoons red wine vinegar

1 tablespoon finely chopped fresh mint

1 tablespoon raw honey

1 garlic clove, minced

6 tablespoons extra-virgin olive oil

Kosher salt and freshly ground black pepper

1 small zucchini, diced

1 cup halved cherry tomatoes

2 scallions, thinly sliced

1 (8-ounce) package Halloumi cheese, cut into ½-inch-thick slices

1 Preheat the oven to 350°F.

2 Arrange the walnuts on a sheet pan and cook until lightly toasted, about 8 minutes. Transfer the walnuts to a cutting board and when cool enough to handle, roughly chop.

3 In a medium bowl, whisk together the vinegar, mint, honey, garlic, and 4 tablespoons of the olive oil. Season with a pinch of salt and a twist of pepper. Add the zucchini, tomatoes, scallions, and walnuts and toss to combine.

4 Set a large skillet over medium-high heat. Add the remaining 2 tablespoons olive oil and heat to shimmering, then add the Halloumi in a single layer. Cook, without moving, until golden brown, about 2 minutes. Flip and continue cooking until the second side is browned, about 1 minute.

5 Transfer the Halloumi to two plates, top with the zucchini salad, and serve.

EGGPLANT PARMESAN

SERVES 2

In the summertime, my dad's vegetable garden was the inspiration for many cherished family meals. Few were more eagerly anticipated than my mom's famous eggplant parm, a recipe that I still rely on countless times a year. This is essentially her recipe, except for the panko bread crumbs that I use instead of the traditional bread crumbs. It's so good that you won't even miss the meat! If you want to double—or even triple—the recipe, dig out your largest enameled baking dish and load it up.

9 tablespoons extra-virgin olive oil

1 small yellow onion, diced

2 garlic cloves, sliced

Kosher salt and freshly ground black pepper

2 (15-ounce) cans crushed San Marzano tomatoes

½ cup all-purpose flour

2 large eggs

1 cup panko bread crumbs

1 cup freshly grated parmesan cheese

1 Preheat the oven to 375°F.

2 Set a large saucepan over medium heat. Add 3 tablespoons of the olive oil, then add the onion, garlic, and a pinch of salt. Cook, stirring occasionally, until the vegetables soften, about 5 minutes. Add the tomatoes and season with a pinch of salt and a twist of pepper. Bring to a simmer and cook, uncovered, for 15 minutes. Carefully transfer the sauce to a blender or food processor and process until smooth.

3 Spread the sauce (there should be about 3 cups) evenly over the bottom of a 9 × 13-inch baking dish.

4 Put the flour in a shallow bowl and season with a pinch of salt. Put the eggs in another shallow bowl and beat them lightly. Put the panko and parmesan in a third shallow bowl and stir to combine. Season both sides of the eggplant slices with salt. Working with one slice at a time, dredge the eggplant in the flour, making sure to coat both sides well.

(recipe and ingredients continue)

1 small eggplant, peeled and sliced crosswise into ½-inch-thick rounds (6 to 8 pieces)

8 ounces fresh mozzarella cheese, thinly sliced

½ cup fresh basil leaves, thinly sliced

Shake off the excess. Dip the eggplant into the beaten eggs, allowing the excess to drip off. Finally, lay the eggplant in the panko, turning and pressing to fully coat both sides.

5 Set a large skillet over medium heat. Add 3 tablespoons of the olive oil and heat to shimmering. Arrange half the eggplant slices in a single layer, making sure to leave space between the pieces. Cook, without moving, until golden brown, about 2 minutes per side. When done, transfer the slices to the baking dish. Repeat the process with the remaining eggplant and 3 tablespoons olive oil. Overlap the pieces in the baking dish if necessary.

6 Arrange the mozzarella evenly on top of the eggplant and bake, uncovered, until golden brown and bubbling and the eggplant is soft throughout, about 30 minutes.

7 Garnish with basil and serve.

Snacks

Growing up in Cleveland, there was only one French onion dip that mattered: Lawson's Chip Dip, which was sold at countless area Lawson's convenience stores. I've never stopped loving that creamy, oniony, salty dip, and I even serve my own version of it with the Pork Cracklin's at Mabel's BBQ. That version is a healthier take on it, made with grilled scallions and far less salt. Serve it with an assortment of sliced veggies like celery, carrot, radish, and bell peppers (or ruffled potato chips!). We also came up with a delicious nut butter made from freshly toasted almonds. It is the perfect dip for wedges of crisp apple or pear. And finally, popcorn is one of my all-time favorite sports-watching snacks. If you have never tried sprinkling on some nutritional yeast, your world is about to flip. I combine that umami blast with the subtle heat of ground Aleppo pepper.

TOASTED ALMOND BUTTER

MAKES 1½ CUPS

2 cups almonds

2 tablespoons coconut oil

¼ teaspoon kosher salt

Sliced apples and pears, for serving

1 Preheat the oven to 350°F.

2 Arrange the almonds on a sheet pan and cook until lightly toasted, about 8 minutes.

3 Transfer the nuts to a blender or food processor and pulse until the mixture has the consistency of fine bread crumbs. Add the coconut oil and salt and process until thick and smooth, about 3 minutes.

4 Store in an airtight container for up to 2 weeks at room temperature or 4 weeks in the fridge.

CHARRED SCALLION DIP

MAKES 1 CUP

4 scallions

1 tablespoon extra-virgin olive oil

Kosher salt

1 cup sour cream

½ teaspoon garlic powder

½ teaspoon red pepper flakes

½ teaspoon za'atar

½ teaspoon celery seeds

2 tablespoons finely chopped fresh flat-leaf parsley

Raw vegetables, for serving

1 Preheat a grill or grill pan to medium-high heat.

2 Drizzle the scallions with the olive oil and season with a few pinches of salt. Set on the grill and cook, without moving, until nicely browned, about 30 seconds per side. Transfer to a cutting board. When cool enough to handle, finely chop and set aside.

3 In a medium bowl, whisk together the sour cream, garlic powder, pepper flakes, za'atar, celery seeds, and parsley. Add the chopped scallions and stir to blend. Taste and adjust for seasoning, adding more salt if necessary.

4 Serve with an assortment of raw veggies.

ALEPPO-SPICED POPCORN

MAKES 4 CUPS

2 tablespoons extra-virgin olive oil

¼ cup popcorn kernels

1 tablespoon nutritional yeast

½ teaspoon ground Aleppo pepper

¼ teaspoon kosher salt

1 Set a large saucepan over medium heat. Add 1 tablespoon of the olive oil and heat to shimmering, then add the popcorn kernels. Cover and cook, while frequently swirling and shaking the pan, until the popping stops, about 3 minutes.

2 Transfer the popcorn to a large bowl. Drizzle with the remaining 1 tablespoon olive oil, top with nutritional yeast, Aleppo pepper, and salt and toss to combine.

NO REFINED SUGAR

APPLE CRUMBLE BARS

MAKES 16 BARS

Not only are these the perfect autumn dessert, but because they freeze and travel so well, you can take them anywhere. I like to mix and match different types of apples, like tart Granny Smith and sweet Golden Delicious, to get a more rounded, balanced flavor, but use what you have access to. These also would be amazing made with a combination of pears like Anjou, Bartlett, and Bosc instead of apples. If you want to avoid a tragic mess when cutting the crumbles into bars, wait until they are completely cool (as difficult as that might be).

Cooking spray

1¼ cups old-fashioned rolled oats

1 cup walnuts

1½ teaspoons ground cinnamon

Kosher salt

4 tablespoons raw honey

¼ cup coconut oil (melted if solid)

1 large egg white

½ lemon

2 cups apple cider

3 medium tart apples, peeled, cored, and diced

3 medium sweet apples, peeled, cored, and diced

2 teaspoons cornstarch

1 Preheat the oven to 350°F. Mist an 8 × 8-inch baking pan with cooking spray.

2 In a blender or food processor, pulse the oats and walnuts until the mixture has the consistency of course bread crumbs. Transfer to a medium bowl, add the cinnamon and ¼ teaspoon salt, and stir until well combined. Add 2 tablespoons of the honey and the coconut oil and stir until the mixture has the consistency of a moist crumble. Scoop out and refrigerate ½ cup of the mixture.

3 In a large bowl, vigorously whisk the egg white until loose and frothy. Add the remaining oat mixture and stir to combine. Transfer to the baking pan, gently pressing it into the bottom to form an even crust. Bake until golden brown and set, about 20 minutes.

4 Meanwhile, using a vegetable peeler, carefully pull off 2 long, narrow strips of lemon zest. Squeeze the lemon juice into a small bowl and set aside.

5 Set a medium saucepan over medium heat and add the cider and lemon zest. Bring to a gentle simmer and cook until the liquid has reduced by half, about 10 minutes. Discard the lemon zest. Add the remaining 2 tablespoons

honey, the apples, and a pinch of salt. Cook, partially covered, until the apples soften and the liquid has reduced, about 15 minutes. Remove from the heat and stir in the cornstarch and lemon juice.

6 Pour the apple filling onto the crust, smoothing it out to the edges with a spatula. Sprinkle the reserved crumble over the top. Return to the oven and bake until golden brown and bubbling, about 30 minutes.

7 Let cool completely before cutting into bars. Leftover bars will last up to 5 days in the fridge or 2 weeks in the freezer.

COFFEE AND CHOCOLATE CHIP BLONDIES

MAKES 16 SQUARES

Until our recipe wizard Katie Pickens came up with this dessert, I had zero interest in ever tasting another blondie. Each one that I've tried over the years has been over-the-top sweet and cloying. Not this one, which still manages to indulge one's sweet tooth without going overboard. The dark chocolate and coffee combination is pure genius.

Cooking spray

½ cup extra-virgin olive oil

1 cup coconut sugar

¼ cup pure maple syrup or raw honey

1 large egg

1 large egg yolk

1 tablespoon pure vanilla extract

1½ cups whole wheat flour

1 teaspoon baking soda

1 tablespoon instant espresso powder

1 teaspoon kosher salt

1 cup roughly chopped dark chocolate (70% cacao or higher)

1 Preheat the oven to 350°F. Line an 8 × 8-inch baking pan with parchment paper. Mist the paper and sides of the pan with cooking spray.

2 In a stand mixer fitted with the paddle, combine the olive oil, coconut sugar, and maple syrup and beat until smooth, about 3 minutes. Add the whole egg, egg yolk, and vanilla and blend to combine.

3 In a large bowl, whisk together the flour, baking soda, instant espresso, and salt. Add the dry ingredients to the egg mixture in the mixer and beat until just combined. Stir in the chocolate. Scrape the batter into the baking pan and smooth the top with a spatula.

4 Bake until golden brown and a toothpick inserted into the center comes out clean, about 35 minutes.

5 Let the blondies cool completely in the pan. Invert the blondies onto the counter, remove the parchment paper, and cut into 16 squares. Store for up to 5 days covered in the fridge or 2 weeks in the freezer.

CREAMY COLD-BREW FRAPPÉ

SERVES 2

Thanks to our family's Greek roots, we all grew up enjoying frappés, which are adored throughout that country. Of course we loved them—they are loaded with sugar! Frappé fans can still enjoy that refreshing iced-coffee beverage, but in a healthier package. Heads up: This recipe requires advance prep in the form of overnight-chilled coffee, frozen bananas, and coconut milk ice cubes. The reward is a creamy and satisfying dairy-free shake-like consistency with real coffee flavor thanks to the cold brew. This frappé might not be traditional, but it's still awesome!

2 cups coarsely ground coffee

1⅓ cups unsweetened full-fat coconut milk, frozen into ice cubes

2 ripe bananas, sliced and frozen

4 tablespoons pure maple syrup

2 tablespoons cocoa powder

1 To prepare the cold-brew coffee, combine the coffee grounds and 4 cups filtered water in a jar, cover, and refrigerate overnight. Strain the coffee through a fine-mesh sieve, discarding the grounds.

2 In a blender, add the frozen coconut milk, frozen bananas, maple syrup, cocoa powder, and 2 cups cold-brew coffee (reserving any extra for another use) and process until smooth. Serve immediately.

COCONUT BANANA "CREAM" PIE

MAKES ONE 8-INCH PIE

What happens when you combine coconut cream pie and banana cream pie? You get this dreamy concoction that marries two of my all-time favorite desserts into one glorious new creation. This recipe relies on coconut cream, the thick and velvety stuff that rises to the top of coconut milk cans—once chilled, you can whip it into cream! You can also find cans of straight coconut cream, but many contain added refined sugar that I want to avoid. You'll end up with extra (but thinner than normal) coconut milk after skimming off and using the coconut cream. Use it in smoothies, oatmeal, and soups.

3 (15-ounce) cans unsweetened full-fat coconut milk

¾ cup old-fashioned rolled oats

¾ cup raw cashews or almonds

¾ teaspoon kosher salt

2 tablespoons raw honey

¼ cup coconut oil (melted if solid)

2 tablespoons cornstarch

3 teaspoons pure vanilla extract

⅓ cup pure maple syrup

2 large egg yolks

2 ripe bananas, sliced

1 The night before preparing, place 2 cans of coconut milk in the refrigerator to chill. Do not shake the cans. Leave the third can out at room temperature.

2 Preheat the oven to 350°F.

3 In a blender or food processor, pulse the oats, cashews, and ½ teaspoon of the salt until the mixture is the consistency of fine bread crumbs. Transfer to a large bowl, add 1 tablespoon of the honey and the coconut oil and stir with a fork to combine until it resembles coarse meal. Press the mixture evenly onto the bottom and sides of an 8-inch pie pan.

4 Bake the crust until golden brown, about 20 minutes. Remove from the oven and allow to cool for 15 minutes before filling.

5 Meanwhile, to make the filling, shake the room-temperature can of coconut milk very well, then open and pour it into a medium saucepan. Measure out 3 tablespoons of the coconut milk and add to a small bowl, then whisk in the cornstarch and 2 teaspoons of the vanilla.

6 Set the saucepan over medium heat, add the maple syrup, egg yolks, and remaining ¼ teaspoon salt and whisk to combine. Bring to a simmer, then whisk in the cornstarch mixture and cook, whisking constantly, until the mixture thickens and bubbles, about 3 minutes. Remove from the heat to cool slightly.

7 Pour the filling into the crust, smooth the top with a spatula, and refrigerate for 2 hours to set the filling.

8 For the whipped "cream," without shaking them, open the 2 cans of chilled coconut milk. Remove the thickened coconut fat that has risen to the top of the cans (you will need ¾ cup of cream; reserve the coconut milk that remains for another use). In a stand mixer fitted with the whisk attachment, combine the coconut cream, remaining 1 tablespoon honey, and remaining 1 teaspoon vanilla and whip until light and frothy, about 5 minutes.

9 Arrange the banana slices on top of the pie and spread the coconut cream on top of the banana slices. Refrigerate until ready to slice and serve.

MOLASSES COOKIES

MAKES 36 SMALL COOKIES

As the original Cookie Monster, I approve! These addictive snacks are buttery, satisfying, and impossible to stop devouring. I don't think enough people appreciate and cook with molasses, an ingredient that adds an incredibly rich, warm, distinctive flavor to foods, while dialing back the sweetness compared to maple syrup and honey. This versatile ingredient adds interest to savory foods like breads, grilled meats, and barbecue, too, so grab a bottle!

½ cup coconut oil, at room temperature

¾ cup coconut sugar

¼ cup molasses

1 large egg

2 teaspoons pure vanilla extract

2 cups whole wheat flour

2 teaspoons baking soda

1½ teaspoons ground cinnamon

1 teaspoon ground ginger

½ teaspoon ground cloves

½ teaspoon freshly grated nutmeg

½ teaspoon kosher salt

1 Position oven racks in the top and bottom thirds of the oven. Preheat the oven to 350°F. Line two sheet pans with parchment paper.

2 In a stand mixer fitted with the paddle, combine the coconut oil and ½ cup of the coconut sugar and beat until smooth. Add the molasses, egg, and vanilla and blend to combine.

3 In a medium bowl, whisk together the flour, baking soda, cinnamon, ginger, cloves, nutmeg, and salt. Transfer the dry ingredients to the mixer and blend to combine.

4 Spread the remaining ¼ cup coconut sugar on a plate. Using a 1-ounce scoop, portion the cookies into 36 balls. Roll each cookie ball in the coconut sugar to coat before placing on the sheet pans.

5 Bake one pan on the upper rack and one on the lower rack until just set, about 10 minutes, rotating the pans from top to bottom and bottom to top halfway through baking.

6 Remove from the oven and cool completely on the pans. Store in an airtight container for up to 3 days or freeze for up to 2 weeks.

WHOLE WHEAT OLIVE OIL BUNDT CAKE WITH ROASTED STRAWBERRIES

SERVES 8

We turn luscious roasted strawberries into a jammy, fragrant sauce that makes the perfect topping for a light, heavenly, and barely sweet olive oil cake. If you love strawberries like I do, make a double or triple batch.

Cooking spray or olive oil, for the pan

2½ cups whole wheat flour

1 teaspoon kosher salt

½ teaspoon baking soda

½ teaspoon baking powder

1 cup plus 1 tablespoon raw honey

1 cup extra-virgin olive oil

1¼ cups unsweetened oat milk or other nondairy milk

3 large eggs

Grated zest and juice of 1 orange

1 teaspoon almond extract

1 pound strawberries, hulled and halved

1 Preheat the oven to 350°F. Mist a 12-cup Bundt pan with cooking spray (or brush with olive oil).

2 In a large bowl, whisk together the flour, salt, baking soda, and baking powder. In a separate bowl, whisk together 1 cup of the honey, the olive oil, milk, eggs, orange zest, orange juice, and almond extract. Add the wet ingredients to the dry ingredients and stir to blend.

3 Pour the batter into the Bundt pan and bake until golden brown and a toothpick inserted into the center comes out clean, about 1 hour.

4 Remove the cake from the oven, but leave the oven on. Set the cake aside to cool for at least 30 minutes before inverting it onto a plate.

5 While the cake cools, roast the strawberries. Line a sheet pan with parchment paper. Add the strawberries, drizzle with the remaining 1 tablespoon honey, and shake them into an even layer. Bake until the strawberries soften and begin to release their juices, about 30 minutes. Stir and continue cooking until the berries darken and the juices thicken, about 15 minutes. Remove from the oven and transfer the berries and any accumulated juice to a bowl.

6 Slice the cake into 8 pieces and serve with the roasted strawberries.

PISTACHIO-CHERRY BARK

MAKES ABOUT 30 PIECES

Barks are a fun and simple cooking activity that the whole family can make together in minutes—and then enjoy together soon after making. To keep this recipe on the healthy side, we call for dark chocolate, which not only omits almost all the sugar found in the milky stuff, but also happens to be full of antioxidants. It's tough to beat the one-two punch of dark chocolate and cherries, but any dried fruit would work nearly as well in their place. This bark can be speed-chilled in the fridge if you prefer, but it will likely turn a little cloudy on the surface from condensation, an issue called "sugar bloom." Don't worry, it's only a cosmetic problem and won't affect the flavor.

⅓ cup pistachios

1 pound dark chocolate (70% cacao or higher), chopped

⅓ cup dried cherries, roughly chopped

½ teaspoon flaky sea salt

1 Preheat the oven to 350°F.

2 Arrange the pistachios on a sheet pan and cook until lightly toasted, about 8 minutes. Transfer the nuts to a cutting board and when cool enough to handle, roughly chop and set them aside.

3 Line the sheet pan with parchment paper.

4 In a saucepan, bring 1 inch water to a boil over high heat. Reduce the heat to low, set a heatproof bowl over the saucepan (make sure the bottom of the bowl doesn't touch the hot water), and add the chocolate. Stir until completely melted and smooth, about 3 minutes. Remove from the heat and set aside for 10 minutes to cool and thicken.

5 Spread the chocolate in a thin, even layer on the parchment paper. Sprinkle the pistachios, cherries, and salt evenly across the top and let cool at room temperature for at least 3 hours, but up to overnight. (Alternatively, you can speed-chill the chocolate in the refrigerator for 20 minutes.)

6 Invert the chocolate bark onto the counter, remove the parchment paper, and break it into about 30 pieces. Store for up to 1 week covered in the fridge.

MISO CHOCOLATE PIE WITH SESAME

MAKES ONE 8-INCH PIE

I know that miso, sesame, and chocolate pie sounds as harmonious as a car backfiring, but trust me on this one. This recipe calls for white miso, the more delicate version of the popular Japanese umami bomb. In addition to delivering depth of flavor, the miso adds a faintly sweet, slightly salty component that enhances the dark chocolate. Just wait until after your friends and family taste it and compliment you to tell them what is in it.

Crust

¾ cup old-fashioned rolled oats

¾ cup raw cashews or almonds

1 tablespoon sesame seeds

½ teaspoon kosher salt

2 tablespoons unsweetened cocoa powder

1 tablespoon raw honey

¼ cup coconut oil (melted if solid)

Filling

2 cups roughly chopped dark chocolate (70% cacao or higher)

1¼ cups heavy cream

1 tablespoon white miso

2 teaspoons pure vanilla extract

Pinch of kosher salt

1 tablespoon sesame seeds

1 teaspoon flaky sea salt

1 Preheat the oven to 350°F.

2 *Make the crust:* In a blender or food processor, pulse the oats, cashews, sesame seeds, and salt until the mixture has the consistency of fine bread crumbs. Transfer to a large bowl, add the cocoa powder, honey, and coconut oil, and stir with a fork to combine until it resembles coarse meal. Press the mixture evenly onto the bottom and sides of an 8-inch pie pan.

3 Bake the crust until golden brown, about 20 minutes. Remove from the oven and allow to cool for 15 minutes before filling.

4 *Meanwhile, make the filling:* Place the chopped chocolate in a heatproof bowl. In a small saucepan, bring the cream to a strong simmer over medium heat. Add the miso paste and whisk until completely dissolved. Pour the hot cream over the chocolate and let sit for 1 minute to melt the chocolate. Whisk until the mixture is completely smooth. Whisk in the vanilla and kosher salt.

5 Pour the filling onto the crust, sprinkle the sesame seeds and flaky sea salt around the perimeter of the top, and refrigerate until completely chilled and set, at least 3 hours, but up to overnight. Slice and serve.

PUMPKIN BREAD

MAKES 1 LOAF

This is the healthier version of pumpkin pie: At least, that's what I keep telling myself as I eat slice after slice after slice! While maybe not as decadent as moist, custardy, whipped cream-topped pumpkin pie, this bread does satisfy the craving for warm-spiced holiday treats. I prefer to use maple syrup instead of honey because the woodsy flavor really ties the whole recipe together.

Cooking spray

2 large eggs

1 cup canned unsweetened pumpkin puree

¼ cup unsweetened oat milk or other nondairy milk

1 teaspoon pure vanilla extract

⅓ cup coconut oil (melted if solid)

½ cup pure maple syrup

1¾ cups whole wheat flour

1 teaspoon freshly grated nutmeg

1 teaspoon baking soda

½ teaspoon baking powder

½ teaspoon kosher salt

1¼ teaspoons ground cinnamon

2 tablespoons old-fashioned rolled oats

1 Preheat the oven to 350°F. Line the bottom of a 9 × 5-inch loaf pan with parchment paper. Mist the paper and sides of the pan with cooking spray.

2 In a large bowl, whisk together the eggs and pumpkin until smooth. Add the milk, vanilla, coconut oil, and maple syrup and whisk to combine. Sift the flour into a separate bowl. Whisk in the nutmeg, baking soda, baking powder, salt, and 1 teaspoon of the cinnamon. Add the dry ingredients to the wet ingredients and stir to combine.

3 Scrape the batter into the prepared loaf pan and smooth the top with a spatula. Sprinkle with the remaining ¼ teaspoon cinnamon and the oats.

4 Bake until a toothpick inserted into the center comes out clean, about 50 minutes.

5 Let the bread cool in the pan for at least 30 minutes before turning out onto a plate and removing the parchment. Store in an airtight container for up to 5 days or freeze for up to 2 weeks.

PEANUT BUTTER-CHOCOLATE BROWNIES

MAKES 16 SQUARES

Don't overlook sweet potatoes when you're trying to bake desserts with less refined sugar. Not only do they help cut back on "the white stuff," but sweet potatoes are rich in vitamins and antioxidants. In this vegan recipe, they pair with the nutty peanut butter to create an irresistible new flavor combination.

1 large sweet potato, halved lengthwise

Cooking spray

½ cup pure maple syrup

½ cup natural peanut butter

2 tablespoons coconut oil (melted if solid)

2 teaspoons pure vanilla extract

¾ cup oat flour

½ cup unsweetened cocoa powder

1 teaspoon baking powder

½ teaspoon kosher salt

½ teaspoon instant espresso powder

¼ teaspoon ground cinnamon

½ cup peanuts

¼ cup chopped dark chocolate (70% cacao or higher)

½ teaspoon flaky sea salt

1 Preheat the oven to 375°F. Line a sheet pan with foil.

2 Place the sweet potato cut-side down on the lined sheet pan. Roast until easily pierced by a knife, about 40 minutes.

3 Remove the sweet potato from the oven, but leave the oven on and reduce the temperature to 350°F. Line an 8 × 8-inch baking pan with parchment paper. Mist the paper and sides of the pan with cooking spray.

4 When the sweet potato is cool enough to handle, scoop out the flesh and add it to the bowl of a stand mixer. (Discard the skins.) Beat the sweet potato until smooth. Add the maple syrup, peanut butter, coconut oil, and vanilla and beat until smooth. In a separate large bowl, whisk together the oat flour, cocoa powder, baking powder, kosher salt, espresso powder, and cinnamon. Add the dry ingredients to the sweet potato mixture and blend to combine.

5 Scrape the batter into the prepared baking pan and smooth the top with a spatula. Sprinkle with the peanuts and chocolate. Bake until a toothpick inserted into the center comes out clean, about 40 minutes.

6 Remove from the oven and sprinkle with the flaky sea salt. Allow to cool completely in the pan, about 30 minutes, before cutting into 16 squares. Store in an airtight container for up to 5 days or freeze for up to 2 weeks.

BATCH RECIPES

Batch-prepared foods are designed to make cooking faster and easier for you. Certain items like brown rice, quinoa, stocks, and faux parmesan can be prepared in advance and in larger quantities for cold storage in the fridge or freezer. They hold up well and will translate into big time-savers down the road. On page 250 we have also included a measurement conversion chart that will help you batch up your own recipes, or simply to double or triple any recipe in this book.

QUINOA

MAKES 6 CUPS

For a while there, quinoa was the punchline of a lot of jokes. I think that's because it is often cooked incorrectly, leaving it mushy, bland, and watery. Prepared correctly, quinoa is nutty, delicious, and versatile. I can eat bowls of it just for the taste and texture, but it also happens to be super healthy because it is loaded with fiber and essential amino acids. It's a great addition to salads and stir-fries or served under roasted vegetables or grilled meats. In this cookbook, I add quinoa to the Mushroom Quinoa Omelet (page 19), use it in place of oats in Overnight Quinoa "Oatmeal" with Blueberries and Walnuts (page 20), and employ it as a crispy base to Soft Scrambled Eggs with Kale and Crispy Quinoa (page 27). Make it in big batches, because this superfood is a valuable utility player in the kitchen.

2 cups quinoa, rinsed

Kosher salt

1 In a medium saucepan, combine $3\frac{1}{4}$ cups water, the quinoa, and a good pinch of salt. Bring to a boil over medium-high heat. Stir the quinoa, cover, reduce the heat to medium-low to maintain a gentle simmer, and cook until the quinoa pops open (releasing the circular white germ of the seed) and all the liquid is absorbed, about 15 minutes.

2 Spread the quinoa out onto a sheet pan and allow it to cool before transferring it to an airtight container. Cooked quinoa will last up to 5 days in the fridge.

BROWN RICE

MAKES 6 CUPS

Rice is easily bulked up, which is why I always tend to have some ready to go in the fridge. We all know that steamed rice is a perfect partner for weeknight stir-fries and the star of crispy fried rice dishes, but I also add it to soups and stews and use it as a stuffing for zucchini. For one of my all-time favorite uses, check out the Crispy Brown Rice and Cauliflower with Fried Eggs (page 41). I love white rice just as much as the next person, but brown rice is equally as tasty and packs more health benefits thanks to the presence of the bran and germ, which is stripped from white varieties. As a whole grain, brown rice has more than double the fiber, antioxidants, vitamins, and minerals of white rice.

2 cups brown rice

Kosher salt

1 Fill a large pot with 10 cups water and bring to a boil over high heat. Add the rice and a couple pinches of salt and cook at a gentle boil, covered, for 30 minutes.

2 Drain the rice in a colander and return it to the pot. Cover and let rest for 10 minutes. Remove the lid and fluff with a fork.

3 Spread the rice out onto a sheet pan and allow it to cool before transferring it to an airtight container. Cooked brown rice will last up to 3 days in the fridge.

FAUX PARMESAN CHEESE

MAKES 1¼ CUPS

Lizzie always, always has this indispensable condiment on hand. Because dairy is hard for both of us to digest, we use this magical ingredient to supply that nutty, "cheesy" taste in a variety of dairy-free recipes. We make weekly batches of it to shake over salads, rice dishes, and breakfasts. I admit that nothing can ever replace the extraordinary and singular flavor of real Parmigiano-Reggiano, but this kitchen staple does help to satisfy that desire for dairy.

1 cup raw cashews

¼ cup nutritional yeast

½ teaspoon garlic powder

¾ teaspoon kosher salt

In a blender or food processor, pulse the cashews, nutritional yeast, garlic powder, and salt until the mixture has the consistency of fine crumbs and resembles freshly grated parmesan cheese, about 10 times. Refrigerate in an airtight container for up to 3 weeks.

KALE AND WALNUT PESTO

MAKES 1¾ CUPS

1 cup walnuts

2 cups roughly chopped kale leaves and tender stems

1 garlic clove, sliced

¾ cup Faux Parmesan Cheese (recipe above)

1 cup extra-virgin olive oil

Kosher salt and freshly ground black pepper

1 Preheat the oven to 350°F.

2 Arrange the walnuts on a sheet pan and cook until lightly toasted, about 8 minutes. Transfer the walnuts to a cutting board and when cool enough to handle, roughly chop and set aside.

3 In a blender or food processor, pulse the kale, walnuts, and garlic until the mixture has the consistency of course crumbs. Add the faux parmesan. With the machine running, slowly add the olive oil in a steady stream. Transfer to a bowl and season with a pinch of salt and a twist of pepper.

4 Store leftovers in the fridge for up to 1 week.

MUSHROOM BROTH

MAKES 12 CUPS

For decades I have been a champion of keeping homemade stocks on hand for cooking. These essential building blocks transform lackluster soups, stews, and braises into restaurant-quality meals. But mushroom stock does even more, because it's not only delicious but also contains loads of antioxidants, B vitamins, and potassium. I like to freeze this broth in 1-cup amounts so I can easily grab one or two portions as needed for a recipe.

4 ounces dried shiitake or porcini mushrooms

3 medium carrots, unpeeled and cut into thirds

2 celery ribs, cut into thirds

1 medium yellow onion, quartered

1 head garlic, halved through the equator

1 small knob fresh ginger, unpeeled and sliced

Small bunch of fresh thyme

Small bunch of fresh sage

2 bay leaves, preferably fresh

1 tablespoon black peppercorns

1 tablespoon grated fresh turmeric or 1 teaspoon ground turmeric

In a large stockpot, combine all of the ingredients and cover with 1 gallon (16 cups) cold water. Bring to a gentle boil over medium-high heat. Reduce the heat to low to maintain a gentle simmer and cook, partially covered, for 1½ hours. Strain, chill, and store for up to 3 days in the fridge and up to 1 month in the freezer.

USEFUL CONVERSIONS

Dry Measurements

Cups	Tablespoons	Teaspoons
1	16	48
¾	12	36
½	8	24
⅓	5T + 1 t	16
¼	4	12

Liquid Measurements

(some liquids—like honey or maple syrup—weigh more than others like milk or water)

Quarts	Pints	Cups	Fluid Ounces
4	8	16	128
2	4	8	64
1	2	4	32
½	1	2	16

Weight Conversions

4 ounces = ¼ pound

8 ounces = ½ pound

16 ounces = 1 pound

More Helpful Conversions

1 tablespoon = 3 teaspoons

2 tablespoons = ⅛ cup

4 tablespoons = ¼ cup

1 fluid ounce = 2 tablespoons

1 cup = 8 fluid ounces

1 pint = 2 cups

1 quart = 4 cups

1 quart = 2 pints

1 gallon = 4 quarts = 128 fluid ounces

Dried-to-Cooked Conversions

2 cups dried beans = 1 pound dried beans = 6 cups cooked beans

1 cup dried beans = ½ pound dried beans = 3 cups cooked beans

1 cup dried quinoa = 3 cups cooked quinoa

1 cup dried old-fashioned rolled oats = 2 cups cooked oats

1 cup dried brown rice = 3 cups cooked rice

ACKNOWLEDGMENTS

This book would not have happened without the overwhelmingly positive reception from readers like you who made the first *Fix it with Food* a *New York Times* bestselling cookbook. That response was especially heartwarming because the book was my most personal one to date, since it dealt with my inflammation and pain struggles as a result of two autoimmune diseases. Like that book, this one continues in that vein, while providing countless new recipes for you and your family.

I wouldn't be here without the love and support of my wife, Liz, who is so understanding about the demands of work and travel. Thanks to Mom, Dad, and my grandparents, who inspired in me not only a love of food but a love of people, regardless of their background. Thanks also to Kyle, Krista, and Emmy. Being able to be so close to them on a daily basis not only inspires me but fills my life with a purpose and joy that I didn't know I could have.

Thanks are due to my longtime business partner, Doug Petkovic. You make me crazy most of the time, but I am grateful that you are always there for me in business, recreation, and life in general as a true friend.

Thanks to my culinary director, Katie Pickens, whose painstaking recipe testing guarantees that every dish in this book will come out great. Over the past decade, Katie has become not only a member of the team but also a member of the family.

Thanks to my manager of fifteen years, Scott Feldman of Two-Twelve Management, a real mensch who represents me as though I'm his only client. Nobody understands the food and media arena better than him. Credit goes to Margaret Riley King with William Morris Agency, a team that always manages to ink the perfect deal.

Thank you to my Food Network family for allowing me to teach and, hopefully, entertain people for the better part of twenty years.

This is the sixth book that I've collaborated on with Douglas Trattner, who is not only my coauthor but also a great, funny, and patient friend and who keeps these projects rolling along despite my challenging schedule.

Photographer Ed Anderson, along with Andie McMahon and Devon Grimes, have a knack for capturing the true spirit of a book, while making every dish look as delicious on the page as it does on the plate. It is always a privilege to collaborate with him and his team.

And, of course, Raquel Pelzel, my meticulous editor at Clarkson Potter. Over the course of three cookbooks, it has been her attention to detail that has resulted in such amazing finished products.

INDEX

Note: Page references in *italics* indicate photographs.

Library of Congress Cataloging-in-Publication Data
Names: Symon, Michael, 1969–author. | Trattner, Douglas,
    author. | Anderson, Ed (Edward), photographer.
Title: Fix it with food: every meal easy : a cookbook /
    by Michael Symon and Douglas Trattner ; photographs
    by Ed Anderson.
Identifiers: LCCN 2021010767 (print) | LCCN 2021010768
    (ebook) | ISBN 9780593233108 (hardcover) | ISBN
    9780593233115 (ebook)
Subjects: LCSH: Quick and easy cooking. | Cooking,
    American. | Menus. | LCGFT: Cookbooks.
    Classification: LCC TX833.5 .S978 2021 (print) | LCC
    TX833.5 (ebook) | DDC 641.5/12--dc23
LC record available at https://lccn.loc.gov/2021010767
    LC ebook record available at https://lccn.loc.
    gov/2021010768.

ISBN 978-0-593-23310-8
Ebook ISBN 978-0-593-23311-5

Printed in China

Photographer: Ed Anderson
Food stylist: Lillian Kang
Food stylist assistant: Paige Arnett
Prop stylist (CA): Glenn Jenkins
Prop assistant (CA): Bill Samios
Prop stylist (NY): Maeve Sheridan
Recipe tester: Katie Pickens

Editor: Raquel Pelzel
Editorial assistant: Bianca Cruz
Designer: Rae Ann Spitzenberger
Art director: Stephanie Huntwork
Production editor: Joyce Wong
Production manager: Kelli Tokos
Composition: Merri Ann Morrell and Hannah Hunt
Copyeditor: Kate Slate
Indexer: Elizabeth T. Parson

10 9 8 7 6 5 4 3 2 1

First Edition